discover the fun of Cake Decorating

Printed and bound in the United States of America

FIRST PRINTING: 50,000
SECOND PRINTING: 35,000

Library of Congress Catalog Card Number: 79-11150
International Standard Book Number: 0-912696-15-X

Library of Congress Cataloging in Publication Data

Main entry under title:
Discover the fun of cake decorating.
    Includes index.
    1. Cake decorating. I. Sullivan, Eugene T.,
II. Sullivan, Marilynn.
TX771.D47   641.8/653   79-11150
ISBN 0-912696-15-X

A message for you:
Here is a book that will open a whole new world of pleasure to anyone who admires the culinary artistry that goes into a beautifully-decorated cake. Perhaps you have been too timid to believe this highly rewarding art form can be mastered by anyone who wishes to do so. We assure you that anyone who is willing to put just an average amount of time and effort into it can learn by following the time-saving Wilton Way.

Discover the Fun of Cake Decorating was conceived and produced expressly for those whose decorating skills may have never gone beyond topping a chocolate-iced cupcake with a cherry. To start your pleasant learning experience you will need very few tools, and many of these will already be within easy reach right in your own kitchen.

As a beginner you need only remember that everything set forth in this unique book is something well within your capacity. You learn the fundamentals of decorating step by easy step and practice with the aid of the carefully detailed, pictures in full color.

To get started you will need comparatively little material you do not already own. For any decorating items you may need, please visit your local Wilton dealer—or write directly to us at Woodridge, Illinois.

Happy decorating!

VINCENT A. NACCARATO
PRESIDENT, WILTON ENTERPRISES

discover the fun
of
Cake Decorating

EDITED BY EUGENE T. AND MARILYNN C. SULLIVAN

WILTON ENTERPRISES, A DIVISION OF THE PILLSBURY COMPANY
WOODRIDGE, ILLINOIS

Cake decorating is fun! You'll gain a wonderful sense of pleasure and satisfaction in creating a lovely little art object. And when you see a child's eyes light up at the sight of his very own birthday cake, you'll know the joy of cake decorating.

Decorating is a craft that anyone with a sense of beauty and dedication can learn. I know, because I've taught it to thousands of students. I promise you that if you study and practice the lessons in this book, you'll be able to decorate a lavish wedding cake like those in Chapter Thirteen, even if you've never decorated a cake before.

Yes, it does take practice. Decorating, like any other art form, aims at perfection and only practice will enable you to achieve the colorful baroque beauty of a well decorated cake. But your enjoyment, and that of those who view and sample your creations will make your hours of practice immensely worth while.

May I make a request? After you've had the fun of browsing through the portfolios of cake portraits in Chapters One, Five and Thirteen, please study the chapters one by one in the order they appear. You'll learn the easy way, by doing. Each chapter explains a special technique and then shows you just how to use your new skill in decorating pretty cakes.

No other art form gives so much pleasure for such a small investment in tools. Some you probably already have, others are available in department stores and cake shops. If you have difficulty obtaining any supplies you may need, please write to Wilton Enterprises, 2240 West 75th Street, Woodridge, Illinois 60515

Best wishes as you begin your adventure in cake decorating!

NORMAN WILTON

DISCOVER THE FUN
OF CAKE DECORATING

Decorating Consultant: NORMAN WILTON
Senior Decorator: MICHAEL NITZSCHE
Decorators: AMY ROHR, DONG TUY HOA
and DONG QUY NHUNG
Art Assistant: SANDRA LARSON
Production Assistant: ETHEL LaROCHE
Photographer: EDWARD HOIS

CONTENTS

CHAPTER ONE

A portfolio of bright birthday cakes

Here's a little gallery of that best cake of all—the birthday cake! It's really the centerpiece of the whole celebration. Browse through this chapter to see all the decorative effects that skillful piping and a beautiful use of color can achieve. Study the chapters on techniques—then decorate a special cake for a dear person's birthday. Watch his eyes light up when you bring in your creation, candles blazing. You'll really know the joy of cake decorating!

This sunny golden cake is very easy to do—even if you've never decorated before, you'll be able to achieve it easily after studying only Chapters Two and Three.

Start by baking a two-layer 9″ or 10″ cake in the birthday child's favorite flavor. Fill the chilled layers, then ice the cake smoothly as page 25 shows. Snow-white Buttercream, page 22, is used for covering and all trim on this cake. Tint it a warm yellow, then ice the cake. Divide remaining icing into three small containers. Add a touch of red to one to make orange, blue to another for green leaves and brown to make gold color. Keep containers tightly covered.

Make seven small decorating cones from parchment paper (page 28), and get out the tubes shown below.

Pipe a few lines of icing on the back of a cookie sheet, and cover with wax paper. Pipe about two dozen orange rosettes and a dozen gold rosettes with tube 21 on the paper and place the cookie sheet in the freezer. They will freeze in just a short time.

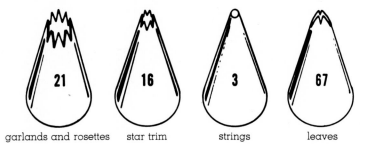

| **21** | **16** | **3** | **67** |
| garlands and rosettes | star trim | strings | leaves |

1. Place the iced cake on a serving tray or foil-covered cake board securing it with a few strokes of corn syrup. If you'd like to add the fluffy touch of a ruffled edging, push the sewn edge of the ruffle under the cake with a small spatula. Divide the top edge of the cake into twelfths and mark the divisions with a toothpick. (Page 42 shows how). Fit a decorating cone with tube 21, fill with yellow icing and begin!

Pipe rosettes all around the base of the cake, setting them close together. Use gold icing and tube 16 to set a little star in each rosette. You've made a very attractive border!

2. Use tube 21 again to pipe the puffy garlands from mark to mark on top edge of the cake. Start with very light pressure and a zigzag motion. Increase pressure and lift the tube slightly as you approach the center of the garland, then decrease pressure as you near the second mark.

Using tube 3, drop curved orange strings from the intersections of the garlands. With gold icing and tube 3, go back and drop a second row of strings below the first.

3. Pipe leaves in groups of three with slightly thinned green icing and tube 67. Lift the tube as you stop pressure to give them a perky point. Press a made-ahead rosette into each leaf group.

4. Lightly mark a circle in the center of the cake with a cookie cutter about 4″ in diameter. Pipe a dab of icing on the back of each rosette and set on the circle, alternating gold and orange. Attach a few more rosettes in the center of the circle. Trim the rosettes with tube 67 leaves. Press birthday candles into the rosettes, letting them extend into the cake surface. (The rosettes will have thawed in just a few minutes.) You've completed a brilliant centerpiece for a happy birthday celebration! Cut this treat into twelve big servings.

This is a very versatile cake design. Wouldn't it be perfect for a lady's birthday in tints of pink? Since we believe that no one should have more than 21 candles on her cake, use just enough to give a festive sparkle.

Yes, hearts and flowers do belong on a cake for a man—and they needn't look too frilly and feminine. Decorate one of these cakes for his birthday. Bake it in his favorite flavor, ice it with luscious Chocolate Buttercream and present it with pride!

Give Dad your love, expressed in a chocolate cake!

Dozens of drop flowers in lively hues shape the hearts on this handsome cake and bright red candles light up the party. This is an impressive creation, very easy to do.

1. Make the drop flowers in royal icing first. You can pipe them weeks ahead, if you like, they keep almost indefinitely. Use tubes 35 and 225 to pipe them. Page 94 shows the easy technique. Pipe a tube 3 dot in the center of each and dry.

2. Bake a two-layer cake in 10" round pans. Make sure the layers are about 2" deep. Chill the layers, then fill and ice smoothly in Chocolate Buttercream (page 22) and set on a 14" cake board or serving tray.

3. Now pipe a border of big puffy shells around the base of the cake with tube 32. Fit a small decorating cone with tube 16, fill with rosy buttercream and frame the shells. Tuck the tube into the space between two shells and draw it around in a curve. Continue until all shells are framed. Mark a curve about 1" in from the edge on cake top, and use tube 3 to pipe the birthday message. Add a tube 16 top shell border.

4. Using patterns in Appendix, starting on page 162, mark the hearts on the top and side of cake, lining up points of hearts. Write "Dad" in side heart with tube 3, then outline the heart with flowers, attaching each with a dot of icing. Outline the heart shape on top of the cake with flowers, then fill it in with more flowers, securing with dots of icing. Insert birthday candles, following the curve of the heart. Serve to 14 guests.

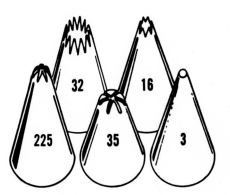

Use tubes 225 and 35 for the drop flowers, tubes 32 and 16 to pipe the borders

Chocolate roses trim a lavish cake

Here's a creation with a continental flair that your man is sure to love. The side borders look intricate, but they're really quick to pipe.

1. First make the roses. Use Chocolate Buttercream, page 22, stiffened with a little confectioners' sugar, tube 104 and the directions on page 101. Make a few rosebuds by stopping with step four of the directions. Let the roses air dry, or if the weather is humid, freeze them.

2. Bake a two-layer 10" square cake. Make sure the layers are approximately 2" high when baked, to allow room to pipe the side border. Fill the cake, then ice the sides with Chocolate Buttercream. Make the recipe for Snow-white Buttercream, but substitute butter for shortening and omit the butter flavoring. Use this to ice the top and for all borders. Set iced cake on a 12" foil-covered cake board.

3. Pipe a tube 19 rosette border at base of cake. Now mark the side border. Use the heart pattern in the Appendix, starting on page 162. (It's easier to mark the sides with a 2" heart cookie cutter.) Mark four hearts on each side of the cake, keeping them evenly lined up about ½" above the border. Pipe an upright shell in the center of each marked heart with tube 17. Starting at the base of the heart, press to form a curved shell, and move up to the point, keeping even pressure. Repeat to pipe other side of heart. Pipe a long curved shell on either side of the point. Twirl a rosette where the two shells meet. You have completed an elegant side border.

4. Pipe the script on the cake top in chocolate with tube 3. Pipe an arc of icing with tube 17 to describe the position of the flowers. Push a tall taper into cake, then arrange the roses, raising those at the back on mounds of icing. Finish the garland with a few tube 67 leaves. (Frozen roses will thaw in just a few minutes.) Serves 20 guests.

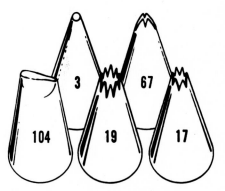

Star tubes pipe the borders, tubes 104 and 67 form the garland, tube 3 does the script

For a child there's no bigger celebration in the year than his birthday—it means just as much as Christmas, maybe more. He'll love to help you with the all-important cake—deciding on the flavor and color scheme, stirring the batter and licking the bowls.

Add the surprise of a little figurine to the cake top, just before the candles are lit. He'll treasure it always as a reminder of a perfect party.

A little garden of a cake charms a girl

Just as pretty as she is and very quick to decorate! Make the dainty drop flowers for the garlands several days in advance with tube 225 and royal icing. Add tube 2 centers. (See page 94). Pipe royal icing rosettes with tube 21 on wax paper and immediately push a birthday candle into each one. Dry flowers and rosettes.

1. Bake a two-layer 8″ square cake, fill and ice smoothly with buttercream. Divide top edge of each side into thirds and mark with a toothpick (page 42). Set the cake on a serving tray.

2. Pipe a tube 21 base shell border. Now drop string guidelines for the flower garlands with tube 2 as shown on page 34. Attach the flowers on the guidelines by piping a dot of icing on the back of each. Add curves of dots below garlands with tube 2. Frame the cake top with a little plastic garden fence, then put the candles in position. Use icing to secure the fence posts and candles. Just before bringing in the cake, add a little plastic figure of a girl and a sprinkling of more flowers. Serve to twelve admiring guests.

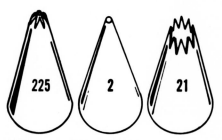

Bring out three tubes to decorate the garden cake. Have decorating cones ready

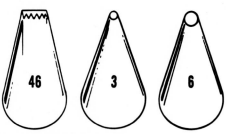

Light up a jolly clown cake to delight a boy

Here's a cake just as happy and bright as the big day. We set a cute little clown figurine on it to tip his hat to the birthday child.

1. As with most decorated creations, some of the work is done in advance of decorating day. Do the letters for "Happy Birthday" and the child's name in Color Flow. Chapter Nine, starting page 115 explains this easy technique. To give the letters a curved shape to conform to the curve of the cake, tape the patterns to the side of a 6″ cake pan, then tape wax paper smoothly over them. An easier way is to use a curved plastic form in the 6″ size. Let the letters dry 48 hours.

2. The cake is a generous size for a big party—it will slice into 20 servings. Bake a two-layer tier in 6″ round pans, and a two-layer tier in 10″ round pans. Fill and ice with buttercream as Chapter Two directs. Set 10″ tier on a 12″ cake board or tray.

3. This is a quick cake to decorate. Divide the top edge of the 10″ tier into twelfths. Page 45 tells how. Press a clean ruler or piece of stiff cardboard into cake surface to connect the opposite marks on the cake top. Now pipe "spokes" on the marks with tube 46. Outline the spokes with tube 3. Center the 6″ tier on the 10″ tier. Mark its top edge, using the spokes on the 10″ tier as guides. Drop tube 3 single strings on the top tier and double strings on the lower tier. See page 34.

4. The cake is finished with ball borders, piped from base to top with tube 6. Add birthday candles in push-in holders, set the clown on top and light the candles! Serves 20.

Basket-weave tube 46 pipes the spokes, tube 3 makes the strings and tube 6 adds the puffy borders

It's always fun to decorate a cake for a lady's birthday—you can indulge in all the ruffles and flourishes created so easily in icing, and satisfy your love for mouth-watering colors and dainty details.

Lattice trims a blossoming heart cake

Airy lattice and brilliant flowers give a summery touch to a love-shaped cake. You'll find this cake very quick to decorate.

1. First pipe the wild roses in varied rosy hues. Use royal icing, tube 103 and the directions on page 97. When you've completed piping the petals, pull out the center stamens with tube 2. Set the flowers aside to dry.

2. Use buttercream for icing and decorating. Bake a two-layer cake in 9″ heart-shaped pans. Fill with her favorite filling and ice smoothly. When icing has set, do the lattice on the cake top with tube 46. Pipe it just as shown on page 46, but since you're using a large tube, you'll find it covers the cake very quickly. Start at the edge of the curve of the heart and draw a line diagonally across to the opposite edge. Leave a space about ½″ and pipe a second parallel line beside it. Continue until you have filled in half the surface, then fill in the other half, starting with a parallel line adjacent to the original one. Now cross the lines in the same manner, keeping them at right angles to the first set of lines.

3. Pipe a base border of puffy shells with tube 32. You'll find directions for this border on page 38. Use tube 103 for the ruffled frame. Now pipe a simple shell border on the top edge with tube 17. Arrange the flowers on the cake top, piping a dot of icing on the back of each to secure. Give some flowers a little more height by setting them on a mound of icing piped on the cake. Trim with a few perky leaves piped with thinned buttercream and tube 65. Complete the summery scene by inserting birthday candles in holders. Serve to twelve.

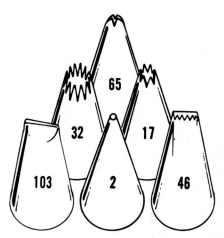

Tubes 103 and 2 pipe the colorful wild flowers, tubes 46, 32 and 17 do the lattice and borders

Pink, pretty and lavished with lace

Lavish curves, dainty lace and fluffy sweet peas come together in a birthday cake that's fit for a princess. It's an elegant cake, but step-by-step, it's quite easy to decorate.

1. Make a royal icing sweet peas first with tube 103 and the directions on page 96. When you tint the icing, do not mix the color thoroughly, leave it a bit streaky. The petals will pipe out in varied tints. Set aside to dry.

2. Bake a two-layer cake in 10″ round pans. Make sure the layers are approximately 2″ high. Fill and ice the chilled layers with buttercream and set on serving tray.

Mark the patterns on the cake. Use the pattern in the Appendix, starting on page 162, for the cake side, transferring it four times to completely circle the cake. For the scallop design on top, cut a 9″ parchment paper circle and fold it into twelfths. Make a pencil mark about 1¼″ in from the edge of each folded side. Cut a curve from mark to mark. Open the circle and trace on cake top. Page 45 shows this pattern-making technique.

3. With tube 1, fill the marked areas with cornelli lace. Page 49 gives a close-up picture. Pipe curved lines, close together, but never touching, until entire space is covered. Cornelli gives a veil-like softness to the cake. Pipe base border exactly like the one on the heart cake, above.

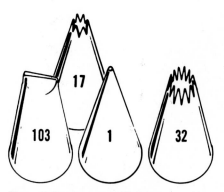

Pipe delicate cornelli lace with tube 1, use star tubes for borders and tube 103 for flowers and trim

4. Pipe the scallops on the side with tube 17. The technique is similar to piping a curved shell as shown on page 33. Start with the curl at the end of a scallop, press heavily to let icing build up, then relax pressure and move down to center of curve. Repeat this movement in reverse on the other side of the scallop, joining smoothly at the center. Do the scallops on top of the cake the same way.

Pipe dots of icing on the backs of the made-ahead sweet peas and press to cake side below scallops as picture shows. Insert tall tapers into cake and add more sweet peas on mounds of icing. Serves 14 guests.

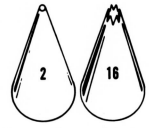

Tube 16 pipes the panda's fur

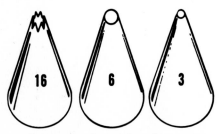

Just two tubes edge the wagon
Pipe your greeting with tube 3

Decorate the panda first

He's really easy to do. Bake a cake in the two-piece panda pan, using a firm pound cake recipe. Chill the cake, set it on a 6″ cake circle and ice with thinned buttercream (page 22).

1. Outline all color areas with tube 2. Be sure to outline the eyes and nose too. Now fill the areas with tube 16 stars. Use Chocolate Buttercream for the brown areas, Snow-white Buttercream for white areas.

2. Thin a little of the icings with corn syrup to consistency of cream and paint in the eye and nose areas with a small artist's brush. Tint a little of the white thinned icing pink and brush in the soles of the feet. Dry.

Now do the red wagon

1. Bake the four cookie wheels first. Use the recipe on page 18, or your own favorite. Roll the dough out about ½″ thick and cut with 2½″ round cutters. When baked and cooled, paint with thinned Color Flow icing (page 116) and dry on wax paper. After they are thoroughly dry, mark a circle about 1¾″ and another about ¾″ in the center of each wheel. (Cookie cutters make this easy.) Outline and fill in the circles just as directed on page 116. Dry about 24 hours.

2. Bake a single-layer 9″ x 13″ sheet cake, chill and set on a cardboard cake base the same size. Ice smoothly with red-tinted buttercream. Pipe a zigzag border at base with tube 16. Run a line of icing around top edge with tube 6, then add a tube 16 zigzag on top of the line.

Assemble the cakes as diagram shows

1. For easy carrying, set this creation on a 12″ x 18″ double-thick cake board, covered with foil. Use royal icing as glue to secure all pieces. First ice a 6″ x 10″ block of styrofoam, 1″ thick, with royal icing. Dry and attach to cake board. Set the wagon on the block.

2. Gently press a 6″ cake circle on the top of the wagon to mark position of panda. Remove, and insert four ¼″ dowels into wagon within the marked circle. Clip off dowels level with top surface (page 146). Dowels will support the weight of the panda. Set panda on wagon.

3. Attach wheels to cake board and wagon with small mounds of royal icing. Pipe your birthday message with tube 3 and fill the wagon with candy. For the handle, push a 9″ length of ¼″ dowel rod into styrofoam block. Cut the wagon into twelve pieces, and the panda (if you can bear to cut him) into twelve pieces.

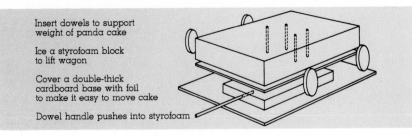

Insert dowels to support
weight of panda cake

Ice a styrofoam block
to lift wagon

Cover a double-thick
cardboard base with foil
to make it easy to move cake

Dowel handle pushes into styrofoam

Surprise the birthday child! Roll in a loveable pet on a coaster wagon

**In a hurry?
Bake a birthday cake
in a pretty shape,
trim it with
made-ahead flowers**

It's fun to spend an hour or two piping colorful royal icing flowers. After they're dried, store them in a covered box. They'll be ready whenever you need to produce an impressive cake in just a short time.

Edge a petal-shaped cake with flowers

Here's a cake that couldn't be easier to turn out. Flower-shaped candles repeat the curves of the cake, bright, quick-to-pipe drop flowers are heaped at the base.

1. Pipe the flowers ahead with tube 35 and royal icing. Add tube 2 centers and dry. See page 94 for easy directions. Bake a two-layer cake in 9" petal-shaped pans. Chill the layers, fill and ice with buttercream. Set on serving tray.

2. Pipe a tube 21 shell border around the top edge of the cake. At the eight points of the petal shapes, pipe single shells, tails pointing inward. No base border is needed. Edge the bottom of the cake with the flowers, piping a dot of icing on the back of each to attach. Arrange the candles on the cake top, light them and present to the birthday child. Serves eight generously.

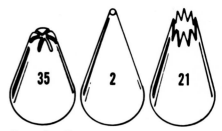

Pipe the flowers in advance. Just one border is needed

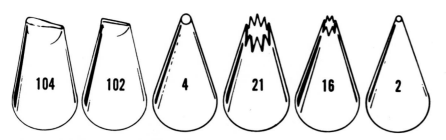

Double daisies garland a hexagon cake

The six sides of this cake show off to perfection the garlands of frilly double daisies. It's an easy cake to decorate—the shape does all the measuring for you and the unusual flowers are piped quickly.

1. First pipe the double daisies. Use tube 104, royal icing and the directions on page 97. Do not add centers—just let the flowers dry flat. Now pipe an equal number of daisies with tube 102. Pipe yellow centers with tube 4 and flatten with your fingertip. Slide the flowers into a curved form to dry. Put the flower together by piping a tube 4 dot in the center of a flat daisy and pressing a curved daisy on top of it. Presto! a frilly flower with extra charm!

2. Bake a two-layer cake in 12" hexagon-shaped pans. Chill the layers, then fill and ice with buttercream. Set on a hexagon-shaped cake board, cut 1" larger than cake all around.

3. The decorating is easy. With tube 21, pipe an upright shell at each corner at the base of the cake, tail extending upward. Use tube 16 to finish the base border with stars (see page 35). Pipe more stars up each corner. Drape a tube 2 string from the top edge of the corners of the cake. This will be a guideline for the flower garlands. Make a mark with a toothpick about 1" in from each corner. Drop a string drape from these marks, then two more within it, keeping the strings parallel. Add top star border with tube 16.

Make the fluffy garlands by piping dots of icing on the backs of the flowers and pressing them to the string guideline. Insert candles in holders and push into top of cake. Surround them with more flowers on dots of icing. Serve this feminine creation to 20 birthday party guests.

Simple borders and draped strings finish the cake

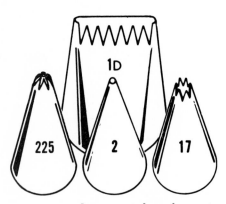

*Just two tubes decorate
the cake, tubes 225 and 2
make the strawberry flowers*

ROLL-OUT COOKIES

1¼ cups butter
2 cups sugar
2 eggs
5 cups flour
2 teaspoons baking powder
1 teaspoon salt
½ cup milk
¼ teaspoon grated orange peel

Cream butter and sugar together, then add eggs and orange peel and beat until fluffy. Sift dry ingredients together and add alternately to creamed mixture with milk. If mixture is too sticky, add a little more flour so that it is easy to handle. Roll dough ¼" thick and cut. Bake on an ungreased cookie sheet in a 375°F oven eight minutes or until done.

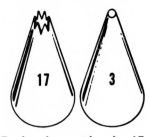

*Do borders with tube 17,
fine trims with tube 3*

These stunning and most unusual cakes are sure to brighten anyone's birthday. The cheerful trims are made in advance—then the decorating is quick and easy.

Clusters of bright red berries . . .

perk up a pretty pink cake—they're made of marzipan and taste just as good as they look.

1. Follow the marzipan recipe and directions on page 85. Tint about three-quarters of the marzipan red, form it into a ¾" cylinder and cut off 1" pieces. Roll each piece in your palms to a rounded conical shape and insert green toothpicks for stems into all but twelve of the berries. Tint granulated sugar red, dampen the berries with a clean cloth, and roll them in the sugar.

To make the leaves, tint the remaining marzipan green and roll it out just like pie dough. Dust work surface and rolling pin with confectioners' sugar. Cut out leaves with a leaf cutter, or use the pattern in the Appendix, starting on page 162. Score veins with a small knife and dry within a curved form as shown on page 104.

Pipe a few tube 225 drop flowers and give them tube 2 yellow centers.

2. To make the cake-top ornament, ice a half-ball of styrofoam, 3" in diameter, with green royal icing. Dry, then insert a tall taper in the center. Insert the toothpicked strawberries and trim with flowers and leaves, securing with a little icing.

3. Now for the cake! Bake two layers in 10" round pans. Fill and ice with buttercream and set on a 12" cake board. Cover the side with tube 1D stripes, drawing them down from the top with cone held straight out. Pipe a shell border at base with tube 17 and use the same tube to pipe the top rosettes, one on each stripe. Attach clusters of berries at the base of the cake with icing and add leaves and flowers. Set the candle cluster on the cake top and call everyone to admire! Serves 14.

Instead of candles, glowing cookie flowers

Here's a really bright new idea for a birthday cake! Bake extra cookies as souveniers for the guests.

1. Bake the cookies first. Use the recipe at left or any recipe that makes a firm cookie. The cookies on this cake take less than one quarter of the recipe. Keep the remainder well wrapped in plastic in the refrigerator.

To tint the dough, knead in liquid food color. Tint a very small portion green, two-thirds of the rest pink and the remainder yellow. We used a 3" flower-shaped cutter with center hole cut out with a 1¼" round cutter, 3" and 1" heart cutters and a 1" leaf cutter.

Cut and bake the hearts and leaves. Line a cookie sheet with foil, shiny side up, coat well with oil and lay the flower shapes on it, each on a damp popsicle stick "stem." Coarsely crush sour ball candies and sprinkle in the circular openings. Three sour balls will fill four cookies. Bake as usual, cool thoroughly and peel off foil. The result—flower cookies with glowing "stained glass" centers!

2. Bake, fill and ice a two-layer 10" square cake. Transfer to cake board and pipe a tube 17 base garland border, then press stars between the garlands. Do the script with tube 3 and the top shell border with tube 17.

Edge the heart cookies with tube 3 beading and use the same tube for script and flowers. Royal icing is best for this. Attach the cookies to cake sides on mounds of icing. If necessary, secure the popsicle sticks to the backs of the flower cookies with a little royal icing, then push the sticks into the cake. Attach leaf cookies to stems with royal icing.

To display this cake at its brilliant best, set it near a window, or place lighted candles behind it. The flowers will glow like jewels! Serves 20.

CHAPTER TWO

Let's prepare for our adventure in cake decorating

Study this book to make your practice easy and fun, your progress fast

Yes, almost anyone can decorate a beautiful cake! What does it take to be a cake decorator? A love of color and beauty and the desire to create a truly original little work of art. Your own two hands and lots of practice in the techniques shown in this book. Practice is essential, for like any other art form, cake decorating aims at perfection and only practice will enable you to create curving sculptural borders, fragile flowers like nature's own, and delicate lace-like string work.

Within each chapter you'll learn basic techniques, then put them right to work to produce a decorated cake you'll be proud of. Many thousands have learned cake decorating the time-saving Wilton-American way. All have achieved a lifetime skill and a rewarding, useful hobby.

Decorating is truly the art that's fun to do and a joy to give!

You'll be well repaid for the time spent teaching yourself to decorate. First of all, you'll experience a wonderful sense of satisfaction in creating with your own two hands a lovely little object. Secondly, and even more rewarding, is the joy you'll receive from giving pleasure to others. Wait till you see a child's big smile when he first sees a colorful birthday cake made just for him, with his own name spelled out. Watch for a man's look of delight when you congratulate him with a luscious cake, done in his favorite colors and flavors.

Many of these tools are already in your kitchen

No other art gives so much pleasure for such a small investment! You'll need just a few special tools to start, none of them expensive.

An electric mixer. Any standard mixer will do, but not a small hand-held model. Later you'll want a heavy duty mixer that will also knead bread and do many other kitchen chores.

Mixing bowls. You'll need one or two large bowls for mixing cakes and icing. A four-quart size is fine. Small plastic containers with tight fitting covers are handy for tinting and storing small amounts of icing. Measuring cups and spoons are also needed.

Spatulas. Get the best quality—a large 11″ size and one 8″ long.

Baking pans. At first, two 9″ or 10″ round pans, a sheet cake pan about 9″ x 13″ and a set of 8″ square pans will be enough. Later you'll want to add pans in unusual shapes, and in a greater variety of sizes.

Parchment paper to make your own decorating cones, and for lots of other uses. 15″ pre-cut triangles are best for making cones, but a 9″ roll is convenient, too.

Cake bases of strong white corrugated cardboard. Purchase these in sizes to match your cake pans, or cut your own.

Food colors. At the start, red, yellow and blue are sufficient, later you'll want to add other hues for speed and convenience.

A strong revolving cake stand, or substitute a sturdy lazy susan, at least 12″ in diameter. This will make it easy to ice cakes smoothly.

Decorating tubes, your most important tools. The assortment on the next page is adequate for a beginner—as you progress you'll enjoy getting acquainted with the scores of other tubes and their interesting effects. Be sure to purchase a number 7 flower nail too.

Get to know your tubes

These little cone-shaped tools of polished metal give form to the icing as you pipe. There are hundreds of tubes, but the ones below are basic, and will decorate almost every cake in this book.

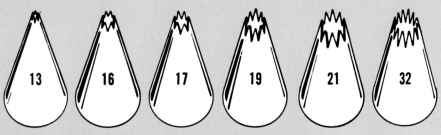

Star tubes are the "work horses" of decorating

As their name indicates, these tubes with serrated openings pipe star-shaped forms as you can see on the border at the top of page 36. But that's just the beginning. They also pipe shells in several variations, garlands, rosettes, fleurs-de-lis and realistic "rosebuds". You can even do block letters and weave a basket with star tubes.

Open star tubes are basic to decorating. Their most frequent use is for piping borders. See two pretty cakes on page 37

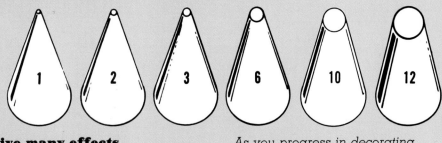

The versatile round tubes give many effects

The plain round openings on these tubes will pipe a line or a bead of icing. Use the smaller ones for script, printing, delicate string work, dainty lace effects and stylized flowers. The larger round tubes pipe garland and ball borders, bunches of grapes and other fruit and even upstanding figures. See cakes decorated only with these tubes on page 48, and beguiling teddy bears on page 112.

As you progress in decorating you'll find many uses for the plain round tubes

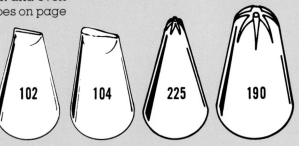

Petal tubes create a garden of flowers

Tubes 101s to 104 are popularly called *rose tubes* but they'll also pipe a host of other flowers. Use them also for rippled borders and bows. Tubes 102 and 104 are the most used sizes. Tubes 190 and 225 make quick one-squeeze drop flowers.

Sweet peas, pansies, petunias and daffodils are all piped with "rose" tubes

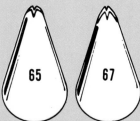

Leaf tubes give flowers a frame

The notched openings on these tubes pipe perfectly formed leaves, from little to large. They'll also make a bluebell or a ruffly border.

Leaves are quick and easy to pipe with these tubes

Icing is the basic material of the decorator

Icing is the edible (and delicious) material from which you create all the fanciful curves and arabesques that make a beautiful decorated cake—so it's essential to choose the right icing for the job at hand.

It's just as important to be sure the *consistency of the icing is correct.* Unless the icing is stiff enough to hold the curve of a petal, thin enough to pipe pointed leaves and just the right texture for crisp borders, you'll never achieve satisfactory results.

All the tested recipes below are perfect for their special uses. Use them for all the practice exercises in this book. Very quickly you'll become acquainted with their characteristics.

Snow-white Buttercream

The icing you'll use most often. It tints well, covers cakes smoothly, pipes clear borders. Tastes delicious, too. Freeze or air-dry the flowers you make from this icing

⅔ cup water
4 tablespoons meringue powder
11½ cups sifted confectioners' sugar
1¼ cups solid white vegetable shortening, room temperature

¾ teaspoon salt
¼ teaspoon butter flavoring
½ teaspoon almond flavoring
½ teaspoon clear vanilla flavoring

Combine water and meringue powder and whip at high speed until peaks form. Add four cups sugar, one cup at a time, beating at low speed after each addition. Alternately add shortening and remainder of sugar. Add salt and flavorings and beat at low speed until smooth. This icing may be stored, well-covered, in the refrigerator for several weeks, then brought to room temperature and rebeaten. Yield: 8 cups. Recipe may be cut in half—or doubled, using a heavy duty mixer.

If you plan to tint this icing, make it at least four hours ahead, then stir it before using. This will eliminate white spots that may form on the surface. Colors will deepen as the icing ages.

Basic consistency is ideal for most uses. *Thin with two teaspoons of white corn syrup per cup of icing to pipe leaves.* For writing and printing, *thin with one teaspoon of syrup per cup.*

Chocolate Buttercream

An exceptionally good-tasting icing. Fine for borders and covering the cake. Pipe cake-top flowers in advance, then air-dry or freeze

⅓ cup butter
⅓ cup solid white vegetable shortening
½ cup cocoa
½ cup milk

1 pound confectioners' sugar, sifted
5 tablespoons milk or cream
1 teaspoon vanilla flavoring
⅛ teaspoon salt

Cream butter and shortening together. Mix the cocoa and ½ cup of milk and add to creamed mixture. Beat in sugar, one cup at a time, blending well after each addition. Add 5 tablespoons of milk, vanilla and salt and beat at high speed until it becomes light and fluffy. Keep icing covered with a lid or damp cloth and store in the refrigerator. Bring to room temperature and rebeat to use again. Yield: 3⅔ cups.

To pipe flowers, *stiffen with a little confectioners' sugar. Thin with ½ teaspoon white corn syrup* for writing and printing. Do not thin for strings or leaves. Add a speck of brown food color to deepen color.

Meringue Royal Icing

The best icing to use for flowers. Made in advance, they'll keep for months, and can be attached to side of cake or given stems for bouquets. Good for "cementing" sections of sugar molds. Dries too hard for covering cakes

3 level tablespoons meringue powder
1 pound confectioners' sugar, sifted

3½ ounces warm water
½ teaspoon cream of tartar

Combine ingredients, mixing slowly, then beat at medium speed for seven to ten minutes. Be sure all utensils are completely grease-free or icing will break down and become "soupy". Keep covered with a damp cloth as the icing dries quickly. To restore texture, rebeat slowly. Yield: 3½ cups. Do not double this recipe unless you use a heavy duty mixer.

To pipe leaves or fine lacy trim, *thin the icing with one teaspoon white corn syrup per cup of icing. Thin with ½ teaspoon of corn syrup per cup* for writing and printing.

Egg White Boiled Icing

2 cups granulated sugar
½ cup water
¼ teaspoon cream of tartar

4 egg whites (room temperature)
1½ cups confectioners' sugar,
   measured then sifted

Covers the cake very well, but not recommended for borders or flowers. Keep tools grease-free, or icing will break down

Mix granulated sugar, water and cream of tartar in a heavy saucepan and boil to 240°F. Brush sides of pan occasionally with warm water and a pastry brush to prevent crystals from forming. Do not stir. Meanwhile, whip egg whites seven minutes at high speed. Add boiled sugar mixture slowly, beat three minutes at high speed. Turn to second speed, gradually add confectioners' sugar, beat seven minutes more at high speed. Rebeating will not restore the texture of the icing. Yield: 3½ cups. Do not double the recipe unless using a heavy duty mixer.

Quick Poured Fondant

4½ ounces water
2 tablespoons white corn syrup

6 cups confectioners' sugar
1 teaspoon almond flavoring

For covering the cake only. This icing gives a beautiful shiny finish that shows off decorating details

Combine water and corn syrup. Add to sugar in a saucepan and stir over low heat until well-mixed and heated until lukewarm. Fondant must be thick enough so it won't run off the cake but thin enough to be poured. Stir in flavor and food color, if desired. Yields four cups, enough to cover an 8" or 9" cake.

To cover a cake with poured fondant, ice the cake thinly with buttercream. Place it on a cooling rack with a pan or cookie sheet beneath it. Pour fondant over the iced cake, flowing from the center and moving out in a circular motion. Fondant that drips onto the sheet can be reheated and poured again.

Figure Piping Icing

3 cups granulated sugar
⅔ cup water
¼ teaspoon cream of tartar

4 tablespoons meringue powder
⅔ cup lukewarm water
1¼ cups sifted confectioners' sugar

Very easy to handle when piping clowns, teddy bears or other three-dimensional figures. Has a nice glossy finish

Cook the first three ingredients to 236°F. While this mixture is cooking, beat meringue powder with lukewarm water until it peaks. Add confectioners' sugar slowly, then beat at medium speed until blended. Now pour the cooked mixture into meringue mixture and continue beating at medium speed until peaks form. Wrap the bowl with towels wrung out of cold water to cool the icing while you are beating. The quicker the icing is cooled, the better it is. (Note: A heavy duty mixer is needed.) Use immediately. This recipe may be cut in half.

How to bake a cake for decorating

Almost all of your favorite recipes or mixes are suitable for a decorated cake. For cakes in upstanding shapes, such as the cute panda on page 15 and the bunny on page 70, it's best to use a firm pound cake recipe. Here are a few tips to help you prepare a cake that will be a perfect background for your artistry.

Experience will tell you how much batter to use

Most of the filled cakes in this book are two layers, each layer approximately 2" high. This results in a cake or tier 4" high. (An exception: the top tier of a wedding cake is usually 3" high, so those layers should have a height of 1½".) For many cakes, this height is necessary to set off borders and side decorations, so be sure to bake the layers in pans 2" high, and fill them with sufficient batter so the cake will rise to the full height of the pan. Only experience will tell you how much batter to use, for cake recipes and mixes vary widely.

Grease your baking pans well with vegetable shortening, dust lightly with flour and bake as recipe or mix directs.

Make sure your layers are level

Level layers are essential for a professional looking cake. To avoid that "hump" on top, do these three things: first, after pouring the batter into the pan, lift it a few inches and let it drop to the counter. Then swirl the batter from the center to the sides of the pan with a spoon. Finally, pin strips of wet terrycloth around the outside of the pan. Tear the 2" strips from an old towel, wet with cold water and wring them out before pinning them around the pan. This will serve to insulate the sides so the edges of the cake do not bake too quickly, forcing the batter into the center of the pan.

If your baked layer still mounds too high in the center, don't be discouraged. After chilling, it is easy to level the surface with a serrated knife.

When the cake is baked, let it cool in the pan ten minutes, then turn it out on a towel-covered rack. Immediately place a second towel-covered rack on top of layer and turn over again. Cake will be right side up with no rack marks.

Always chill the layers before decorating

Now let the layers chill in the refrigerator for several hours. Or you may freeze them, wrapped in wax paper, then plastic. This allows you to bake days or weeks ahead, and lets you enjoy the fun of decorating without the bother of baking. Remove layers from the freezer, pat dry with a paper towel, and they are ready to ice.

This chilling or freezing gives the layers a much firmer texture and makes them easy to handle and move.

Every cake should rest on a cardboard base

Always attach the cake to a corrugated cardboard cake circle or base. This makes it much easier to move, allows you to separate stacked tiers for serving with ease, and prevents knife scratches on the serving tray. Use a base the same size and shape of the cake, stroke on a little royal icing or corn syrup, and set the layer or cake on it.

Give your cake a smooth coating of icing

Just as a painter needs a well-stretched canvas, a decorator needs a smoothly iced surface to work on. It's really quite easy to achieve—just follow these six steps, and use plenty of icing so all cracks and crevices are filled in.

1. Brush off any loose crumbs from the base layer and set it on the turntable, attaching it with a few dabs of icing. Pipe a ring of icing around the top edge of the layer with any large tube, then spread your filling within it. Almost any filling is suitable, except one made with fresh fruit, which may seep through and discolor the final coat of icing. You may choose to use buttercream or boiled icing as a filling.

2. Brush loose crumbs from the top layer and set it on the base layer. Now give the cake a crumb coating. There are two ways to do this. The continental way is to cover the cake with apricot glaze. Heat a cup of apricot preserves to boiling, strain, and, while still hot, brush it over the cake with a pastry brush. The glaze adds a touch of tangy flavor and dries hard in a few minutes.

The second way is to cover the cake with a very thin coat of whatever icing you are using for the final coating, usually buttercream. Do this with a spatula. This method has the advantage of masking the color of the cake so there is no possibility of it showing through. Let this icing set about ten minutes till a crust forms. Now you're ready to apply the final coat of icing.

3. First cover the side of the cake. Work from the bottom up, using long even strokes and plenty of icing. Build up the icing a little at the top edge of the cake. Let the turntable help you, turning it as you spread the icing. Do not smooth the icing at this time.

4. Now heap icing on the top of the cake and spread it out. Now you're ready to give the cake a smooth finish.

5. Use a strip of stiff clean cardboard to smooth the top. Hold it by the ends and draw it across the cake surface, pulling the excess icing toward you.

6. Now smooth the sides. Hold a long spatula at a slight angle and slowly spin the turntable. Voila! A perfectly iced cake, ready for decorating. Slide a spatula under the cake and transfer it to a serving tray or foil-covered cake board.

How to prepare a cake board

Any pretty tray or cake stand is fine for showing off a cake, but if you don't have one the right size, use a foil-covered cake board. Cake boards are convenient for "give-away" cakes, too. No tray to return! Use a corrugated cardboard cake circle or base about 3" larger than the cake. Purchase foil at a florist supply house. It comes in rolls in many patterns and colors. Cut the foil about 4" larger than the board. For a round board, cut 1" slashes around the edge of the foil. Smooth the foil over the board and tape the slashed edges underneath. Secure the iced cake to the board with a few strokes of icing or corn syrup.

Color, skilfully used, is the most important element on a cake

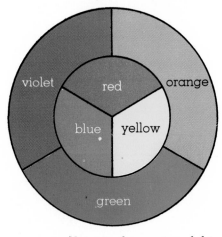

Hues in the center of this wheel are primary colors, those on the outer edge are secondary colors

The three cakes above are almost identical in design and trim—but each has a completely different personality because of its color scheme.

Dainty yellow and white makes a sweet cake for a baby shower. Lime and violet are set off by white borders and accented with turquoise flowers to create a sophisticated birthday cake for a lady. Rose and warm orange are enhanced by mossy green leaves in a glowing cake for the holidays.

Make a few exciting color experiments of your own. Mix up small bowls of icing and tint various hues. With a small spatula, put dabs of tinted icing next to each other on a white cake circle. Deepen some of the tints and make new combinations. You'll be surprised and delighted at some of the effects created. Inspiration for color schemes is everywhere. Study the colors in nature, especially flowers. Look at paintings, fabrics and attractive interiors. You'll gain a new appreciation of color, and decorate more beautiful cakes.

Just a word of caution. Cakes are made to be eaten, so all colors used in decorating must look fresh and attractive. Avoid large areas of deep blue, green or violet—use light tints instead. Grey and black are not appetizing, so avoid using them on a cake.

Paste food colors are the most versatile—you can use them for a dainty tint or a deep rich tone. Caution—these colors are very strong, so use them sparingly! Liquid colors can be used for pastels. The three primary colors in the center of the color wheel will combine to make the secondary colors in the outer portion of the wheel. Red plus yellow makes orange, yellow plus blue, green, and blue and red, violet. All three primary colors will combine to a drab muddy brown.

For convenience and speed, however, decorators prefer to have an assortment of colors on hand. Purchase a basic kit of eight colors, or buy this assortment: Red-Red, Lemon Yellow, Orange, Leaf Green, Pink and Royal Blue. This will be sufficient for almost any need.

Here's the professional way to tint your icing

Let's use the clown birthday cake on page 10 as an example. Mix a recipe of Snow-white Buttercream. Put a small amount in a small container and add just a speck of yellow food color on the end of a toothpick. Mix thoroughly. If the tint is too light, add another speck, until you achieve just the tint you want. Keep the container tightly covered until you're ready to use it. Now tint the main portion of the icing with pink in the same way. Spoon out just a little into a container, and add more pink for the deeper colored string trim.

Always tint Buttercream at least four hours ahead of decorating time, as colors tend to deepen. Store in the refrigerator tightly covered, then bring to room temperature, beat at low speed to original consistency, and you're ready to decorate.

Deep colors make striking accents

Don't feel you need to decorate only in pastels—brilliantly colored accents are beautiful! If you are tinting royal icing in deep hues, just add the paste color, bit by bit, until you achieve the color you want. Long-lasting flowers in bright royal icing are usually saved by guests as souvenirs of the party.

Bright red buttercream flowers sometimes have a bitter taste because of the amount of food color mixed in. Add a little powdered cocoa to improve the taste. And tint your icing a lighter red than the one you want—the color will deepen in a few hours.

Add a professional touch with color striping

Spatula striping pipes a border in interesting varied tints, and gives flower petals a deeper tint in the center. Roll your decorating cone and drop in the appropriate tube. With a small spatula, apply a stripe of tinted icing to the inside of the cone, from the tip to about two-thirds of the distance to the top of the cone. Fill the cone with white icing, or icing in a paler tint. Details will pipe out two-toned.

Brush striping makes vivid borders or realistic pansies. Stripe the inside of the decorating cone with a small artist's brush using paste color right from the jar. To make the three-tone border at right, brush a red stripe on one side of the cone, a green stripe on the opposite side. Fill the cone with white icing.

Spatula striping

Brush striping

*Would you like to make
a cut slice of cake
as pretty as the outside?
Use a white cake recipe
or mix and add a
touch of color to the batter.
Liquid colors are best for this.*

CHAPTER THREE

Let's start working with tubes

First make the parchment paper cone that holds the icing. With just a little practice, you'll be able to make a cone in a minute! Before you start to pipe, make a number of them and nest them together so they're at hand when you want to change colors of icing, or need a fresh supply. Although ready-made decorating bags are available and convenient for large-scale decorating, for most uses we recommend parchment cones. They're sanitary, disposable and never need washing.

All directions in this chapter are for a right-handed decorator. If you are left-handed, reverse the directions.

Use 15" pre-cut triangles of parchment paper to make decorating cones. For tiny cones for small trims, cut the triangles in half

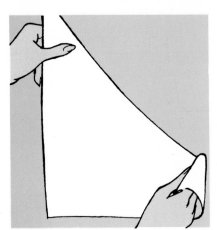

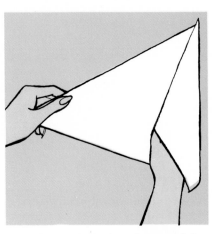

1. Lay the triangle flat on the counter with the longest side away from you. Slide your right hand, palm up, under the right hand point of the triangle and grasp it with your thumb and forefinger, keeping your thumb on top.

2. Roll your right hand toward the center, holding opposite corner firmly with your left hand. The cone will start to form almost automatically.

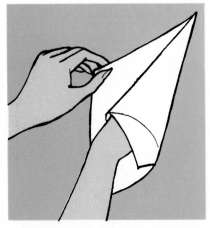

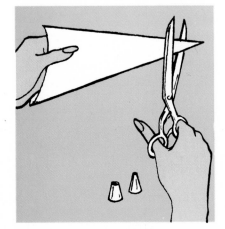

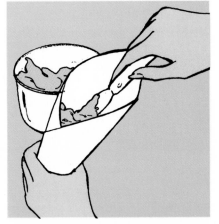

3. Now twirl the left corner of the triangle all the way around the cone. Work it back and forth until the point is needle sharp. Staple the cone near the top, or fasten with a strip of tape.

4. Cut off the tip of the completed cone about ½" from the end. Don't cut off too much or the decorating tube will fall through—you can always trim a bit more. Drop the desired tube into the cone, small end down. About ½" of the tube should be visible, extending from the cone.

5. To fill the cone, hold it with your left hand and use a small spatula to scoop the icing inside. Press the spatula against your left thumb to release the icing. Fill the cone only three quarters full. Fold top edge of cone in a "diaper fold". Fold again to close. Continue folding to force icing into tube, then fold as icing is used.

**Learn to hold the
decorating cone
in the correct position**

To decorate smoothly and easily
and achieve neat, professional
results, it's absolutely essential to hold the cone at the
correct angle. Study the hand
picture on this page and on
pages 30, 31 and 32, and practice until your hand will almost
automatically assume the correct
position for the designs you
wish to pipe. Use buttercream
icing (page 22) in its basic
consistency and work on the
back of a cookie sheet
or on a practice board.

Hold the filled cone in your right hand, thumb on top and point it at a 45°
angle to the base of your cake pan. *45°means midway between horizontal and straight up.* This angle is best for top borders too—it puts the
border on at a slight angle to cover cake edges evenly and gives the
cake a finished appearance. Squeeze the cone with your right hand,
use the fingers of your left hand only to guide the cone.

**Hold the cone at a 45° angle
for most borders
at top and base of cake**

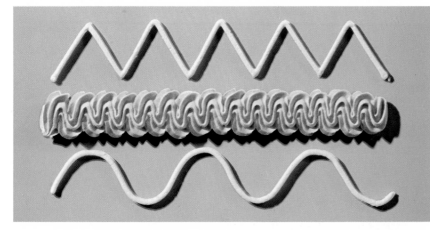

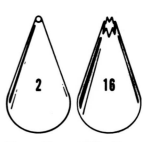

**Practice with the cone
at a 45° angle**

Prop your cookie sheet or board in an upright position and practice
zigzags and curves. Hold the cone at a 45° angle, and make up-and-
down motions to produce a zigzag design with tube 2. Use tube 16 to
make a tight zigzag as shown in the pink design, keeping your up-and-
down motions very close. Now put this border on the base of a round
cake pan as shown in the top picture. See how it fills in the area between
base of pan and flat surface. Use tube 2 again and practice a repeated
curve on your propped-up cookie sheet. Maintain the 45° angle as you
move your hand up and down, keeping the curves uniform.

For lines, script and printing, hold the cone as flat as possible

Straight or curved lines are achieved by holding your cone nearly parallel to the surface. Your left hand will be almost palm up. It's important to barely touch the surface with the tube, just skimming along, and never digging in. After you've practiced the exercises below, you'll be able to pipe curving stems for a flower spray.

Practice piping lines with the cone held almost flat

Use tube 3 for these practice exercises, and do them on a cookie sheet resting on the counter. *Thin the buttercream icing slightly as directed on page 22.* Hold the cone as flat and parallel to the surface as possible and pipe a series of straight lines, first vertical, then horizontal and diagonal. Try to keep them uniformly spaced. Now try curves in opposing directions. Set a round cake pan upside down and pipe a spray of graceful stems as shown in the picture at top.

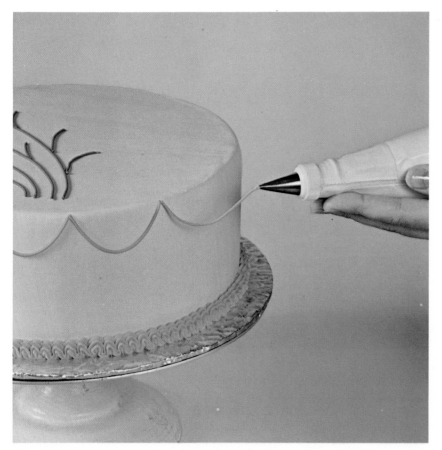

For draped stringwork, hold the decorating cone straight out

String drapes give a lovely lacy look to a cake and are really easy to do. Point the decorating cone straight at the cake surface, and let the string drop by itself. *Never move cone down*, hold it level with the point of attachment. Make sure your work is at eye level—set the cake on a pile of books or sturdy support if necessary to raise it.

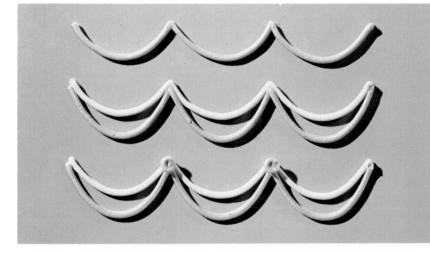

Dropping string drapes is fun! Try these practice exercises

Prop your cookie sheet or board in a vertical position, and make sure it is at eye level. Thin the buttercream as directed on page 22. Using tube 3, and holding cone *straight out*, touch the tube to the surface, squeeze lightly to attach, continue squeezing as you *move out, not down*, come back to surface to attach again. The string will drop by itself in a graceful curve. Practice single and double rows of strings, moving rhythmically to keep the drapes even. Twirl rings at the points.

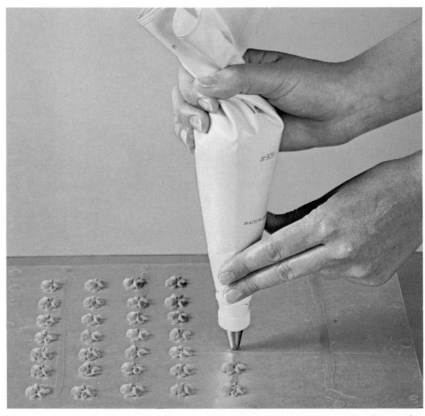

For stars, dots and rosettes, hold the decorating cone perpendicular to the surface

To pipe the designs shown below, the cone is held perpendicular to the surface, and this angle is also correct for the drop flowers shown above. To pipe these forms on the top surface of the cake, hold the cone *straight up*. If you are piping on the side of the cake, hold the cone *straight out*, again perpendicular to the surface. Use buttercream (page 22) in its basic consistency.

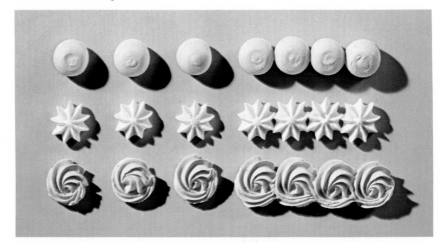

Holding the cone straight up, pipe some basic forms

Practice piping dots with tube 6. With cookie sheet or board lying flat on the counter, *hold the cone straight up*, touch surface lightly and squeeze. As icing begins to mound, raise the tube slightly, stop pressure, then move away. Use tube 16 to pipe stars. Hold cone straight up, touch surface lightly, squeeze, stop pressure and move away. Pipe rosettes with the same tube. Starting in center, squeeze while making a circular motion, stop pressure and move away.

Learn to control your pressure on the cone to assure neat, artistic piping

Your decorating ability will depend on the degree of pressure control you achieve, so please practice the exercises below and on the next two pages diligently. You will learn to exert a gentle even pressure as you move the cone freely across the surface of the cake, and to stop pressure completely to end a design in a clean break.

Practice on the back of a cookie sheet, using basic consistency butter-cream (page 22) unless otherwise noted. Be sure to hold the cone at the correct angle—use your right hand, thumb on top of cone, to exert pressure, and the fingers of your left hand to guide and steady the cone. Let's begin—you'll soon get the feel of it!

Start pressure control practice with the shell—the most basic decorating design

This classic form is used in so many borders and other trims, it's wise to master it at once. Position your cone at a 45° angle to the surface and use tube 21. Touch the surface lightly and press heavily. Let the shell build up as you lift the cone just enough to go along with the icing. Now relax your pressure, pull your hand down abruptly, stop pressure completely and draw away for a clean break.

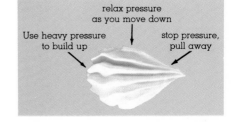

relax pressure
as you move down

Use heavy pressure
to build up

stop pressure,
pull away

Practice variations of the basic shell to learn to control pressure

Any of the star tubes, 13 to 21, may be used for this practice, but here we show tubes 16 and 19, good medium sizes. Hold the cone at a 45° angle to the surface of the pan.

1. Make a row of shells, just as described above. Strive to keep them all uniform in size and shape. Join one on the tail of another to produce a neat shell border.

2. With tube 16 and cone at 45° angle, practice reverse shells. Pipe them just the same as regular shells, but as the shell builds up and fans out, relax pressure and bring your hand in a curve to the right, then stop pressure and move away. Pipe a second shell, curving to the left instead of right. Continue piping curved shells, alternating curves.

3. Use tube 19 and cone at 45° angle to pipe upright shells. Pipe them just as you did the basic shell, but in a vertical position. Set your practice pan upright and join them for a border.

4. Pipe a pretty fleur-de-lis with tube 19. First pipe an upright shell, then add one curved to the left on the left side, one curved to the right on the right side. Now practice them on an upright pan. Fleurs-de-lis make an elegant decoration for the side of a cake.

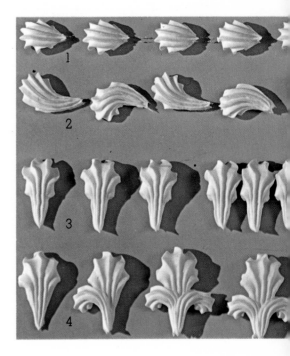

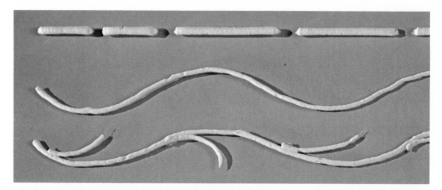

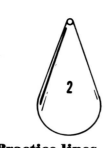

Practice lines, straight or curved

Use tube 2 and *thinned buttercream* (page 22) to practice lines. Use a light, even pressure with the cone held as flat as possible. Touch the surface, lift tube very slightly and let the line drop in place. Touch again, stop pressure and move away. Draw out a curving line, keeping curves evenly spaced. Pull out short curved lines and you've the beginning of a vine border. This practice will help you print and write in icing, too.

Practice puffy garlands

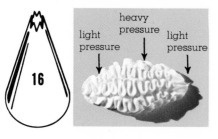

Use tube 16, basic consistency of icing and hold the cone at a 45° angle to the surface. Start with light pressure and an up-and-down zigzag motion. As you approach the center, lift tube slightly and increase pressure to let the icing build up. Decrease pressure as you near the end of the garland. Pipe joined garlands for a dramatic, puffy border.

Practice string drapes

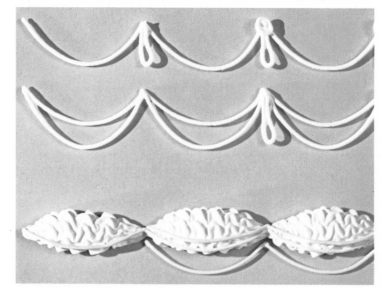

The side of a box or carton offers a good surface to practice on. Use tube 3, and thinned buttercream (page 22). First pipe dots of icing every 1½" on the top edge of the box as spacing guides. Now hold cone straight out, touch to first dot and squeeze lightly to attach. Continuing pressure, move straight out as string drops by itself. Bring tube to second dot to attach. *Never move your tube down* to follow string. Do several rows of string, keeping a steady rhythm so drapes are even. Drop little loops at each connecting point and finish with a little twirl of icing. Drape strings over garlands for a very dressy border.

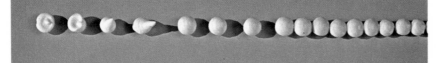

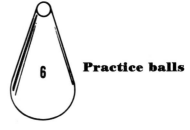

6   **Practice balls**

Use tube 6 and hold the cone straight up. Using a steady, even pressure, lift the tube slightly along with the icing as it builds up, keeping the tip buried. Stop pressure, *then* move away. The first two balls in the picture show the results of not lifting the tube. The second two balls show how points will occur if pressure is not stopped completely *before* moving away. After you have piped a few balls, join some for a border.

PRACTICE STARS AND ROSETTES

32   **Practice stars**

Perfect stars are easy to pipe if you make sure to hold the cone *straight up.* Touch tube 32 lightly to surface, give a quick squeeze to the cone, stop pressure and move away. If the cone was held absolutely straight, the center point of the star will be in the exact center. Pipe stars close together for an effective border.

PRACTICE LEAVES

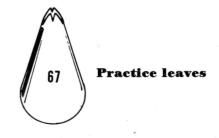

67   **Practice leaves**

To pipe life-like leaves, thin the buttercream as directed on page 22. The cone should be held at about a 60° angle—midway between 45° and 90°. Touch tube 67 to surface, give light pressure, then lessen it as you move. Stop pressure completely, still moving, as you pull the leaf to a point.

Tube 21 makes a pretty border for a cake top—just pipe reverse shells, one on the tail of another around the top edge. Refer to page 33. Practice this on a 10" cake circle, then put it on a cake top. Finish the base with rosettes made with the same tube as shown on page 32.

16

Here's a showy cake-top border. With tube 16 pipe a curved "vine" as shown at the top of page 34. Add short stems, then finish with tube 21 red stars. Try it on a cake circle, then on a real cake. Add a bottom shell border (page 33) with tube 21 and you've completed a very pretty cake!

16   **21**

35

CHAPTER FOUR

The art of beautiful borders

Borders are the abstract icing designs that frame a cake. They are applied to the bottom and top edges to fill in the space between cake and serving tray and give a finish to the top. But borders are much more than that—often they can be the only cake trim as the cakes at right demonstrate. There can be cakes devoid of flowers, but few, if any, without borders. Study this chapter to see how basic forms you already know can be added to and modified to achieve highly original borders.

Just one tube and icing enhanced with color pipes a sparkling border

Here is a border composed only of simple stars, but color and design make it very effective. To practice it, fit a decorating cone with tube 21, spatula-stripe it with deep rose icing, then fill with white. (See page 27.) Holding cone straight out from side of cake, give a quick squeeze, stop pressure and move away to pipe a star. Make a row of stars, set neatly close. Now pipe two stars below the first three, then one below the two. Proceed until you have a border with a zigzag edge. This makes a nice tailored finish for the top of a cake.

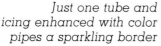

Dress up rosettes with little drop flowers

Tube 13 drop flowers give a sweet finish to a simple rosette border. Hold tube 21 straight out and pipe a row of rosettes, starting in the center and swirling around to make a circle. After you've piped the rosettes, touch tube 13 to the centers, squeeze as you turn your hand sharply to the left, stop squeezing and pull away. A very professional border, quickly done, for top or base of cake.

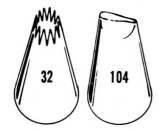

Pipe a basic shell border, then trim it with fans

Here, little fans trim a basic shell border. Start by piping a row of puffy shells with tube 32, keeping them uniformly spaced. Now pipe the fan trim between each shell. Change to a tinted icing and tube 104. Hold cone straight out, wide end of tube at bottom, give a quick gentle squeeze, stop pressure and move away. An effective base border.

At right: two beautiful cakes whose only trim is borders, done with star tubes. You already know all the basic techniques—see pages 43 and 45 to learn how to put them together.

Many borders start with a shell

The beautiful classic form of the shell has inspired many cake borders. A row of simple shells alone makes a good border for many cakes, but variations and added trims offer many decorative possibilities.

Deeply curved shells for a simple but outstanding border

The curves of reverse shells are so rhythmic and beautiful, they're often the only border a cake needs. Review page 33 and pipe a row of connected reverse shells on your cookie sheet. Use tube 21 and the hand position shown on page 29. Make the shells extra puffy by squeezing strongly to let the shell build up and give very sharp clockwise or counter-clockwise motions to create the strong curves. Use this border for either top or base of a cake.

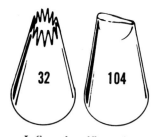

A fluted ruffle softens a simple shell border

Trim shells with curved ruffles for one of the most popular borders ever piped. See it on two pretty cakes, page 12. Start with a row of shells piped with tube 32. Now use tube 104 for the ruffle. Holding cone straight out, tuck the wide end of the tube under a shell, just at the tail of a preceding one. Curve around the base of the shell using even pressure and jiggling your hand slightly to form the ruffle. As you approach the tail of the next shell, relax pressure, then stop pressure and pull away.

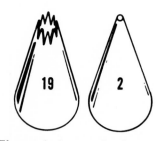

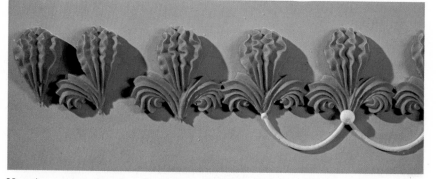

Fleurs-de-lis are the basis for a formal side border

Here's a pretty border, based on the classic fleur-de-lis, to pipe on the side of a cake. First pipe a tube 19 upright shell, cone held straight out, just as shown on page 33. To give the rippled effect, jiggle your hand slightly as the shell builds up. Now pipe a sharply curved shell on either side of it. Use thinned icing and tube 2 for string trim. Hold cone straight out, touch to base of fleur-de-lis, pull away, allow string to drop, then touch to base of next fleur-de-lis. Finish with tube 2 dots.

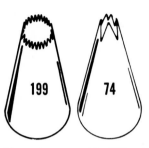

Try using tube 199 for the basic shells on this border, and see how the finely serrated opening gives a very different effect. Pipe a row of shells, using the cone position on page 29. Now frame the shells with tube 74 curves, holding the tube with the deepest groove up. Starting where two shells join, pipe curves on top of all shells, then a second series of curves at the base. Finish by piping tube 4 dots between all shells. This interesting border looks best at the base of a cake.

Experiment with different tubes to pipe a shell border variation

Here's a simple, but very beautiful shell variation border for a cake top. Just one tube is used. With tube 16, pipe a long line of icing. Just above it, pipe a row of shells, keeping them neat, uniform and close together. Now below the line, pipe another row of shells. Finally, pipe a row of shells right on top of the line. The secret of this border is keeping the three rows of shells lined up. To use on a cake, pipe the line at the exact edge of the cake top, then add shells.

Triple shells give a "picture frame" look

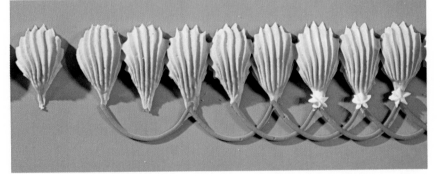

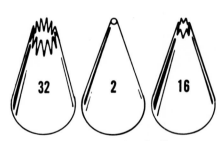

Pipe this border around the top edge of a cake for a regal crown effect. Start by piping a row of upright shells with tube 32, keeping sides touching and holding cone straight out. Use tube 2 and thinned icing to drop a string from the base of the first shell and attach it to the third shell. Keep cone straight out. Go back and drop a string from base of second shell, attach to base of fourth shell. Continue to drop strings to form the interwoven effect. Finish by piping a tube 16 star at base of each shell.

Start with an upright shell, trim with stars and strings, create a stunning border

Use basic icing forms to pipe more borders

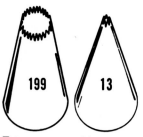

Trim a row of big stars with a contrast frame

Here's a good-looking border based on a simple star, then trimmed. Pipe a row of stars with tube 199, uniformly sized and spaced. Hold cone straight out, barely touching the surface. Squeeze as you lift cone slightly, stop pressure and pull away for a perfect star. Now use contrasting icing and tube 13 to pipe an arch over the top of each star. Add arches below the stars also. This border is best at the base of a cake, but can be used for the top edge, too.

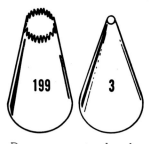

Dress up a star border with dropped strings

This cake-top border is based again on the star form. Pipe a row of tube 199 stars, cone held straight out from surface. Move the cone toward you as the icing builds up for a very raised form, then stop pressure and pull away. Use tube 3 to pipe an "e" motion frame over tops of stars. Repeat the frame below stars. Now drop a shallow curve of string below each star, on top of frame, for a built-out effect. Add a row of intertwined string drapes. Hold cone straight out, attach string to left side of first star's frame, let drop and attach to right side of frame below second star. Drop string from right side of frame below first star and attach to right side of frame below third star. Continue dropping strings as picture shows. This is a fine border for top of a wedding or other large cake.

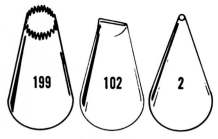

Add ruffles and strings to a shell border

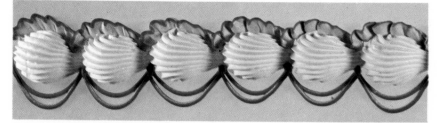

A handsome cake-top border is based on tube 199 shells. Pipe a neat row of them, then add tube 102 ruffles. Brush-stripe the decorating cone with pink color from the jar, then fill with pink icing. (See page 27.) Starting at center of curve of first shell, wide end of the tube next to shell, jiggle your hand as you curve around shell, lessening pressure as you approach the tail of the shell. Repeat for all shells for a rich, two-toned trim. Then with thinned icing, drop a double row of tube 2 strings. Piped on a cake, the ruffle would flare above surface of cake top.

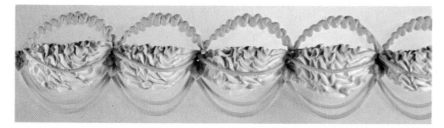

This lovely border uses the garland for its basic structure. Pipe a row of tube 19 zigzag garlands as described on page 34, increasing pressure and lifting tube slightly as you approach center, relaxing pressure and lowering tube as you approach the end of the garland. With tube 3 and thinned icing, pipe an "e" motion scallop above each garland. With the same tube, drop strings across the garlands, and drop double strings below them.

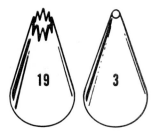

Build a beautiful border on a basic form

Now that you've practiced a few basic borders, you've realized that all borders are based on the basic forms in pages 33 through 35. Now enjoy dreaming up some borders of your own. Here's an example. Pipe a row of hearts with tube 10. The hearts are formed by piping two shells, touching. Pipe a tight zigzag arch over each heart with tube 13. Pipe stars within the arches with the same tube, then two curved shells on top of each heart. Drop a single tube 2 string from base of each heart, then a deeper one from every other heart. Pipe tiny hearts with tube 2 between the large hearts, then finish the border by piping tube 13 stars where the strings join hearts.

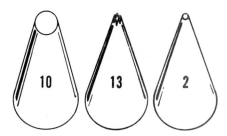

Use basic icing forms to create an entirely new border

How to measure a cake before piping borders

Many cakes require measuring and marking before being decorated so that all the borders and other trim are placed evenly and symmetrically. Measuring a cake is really a very quick and easy job. You don't need a ruler or a tape measure—just strips of paper and your own two hands. Either parchment paper or wax paper is ideal.

Measuring the sides of a square cake

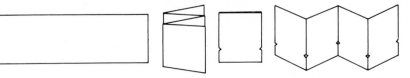

Use parchment or wax paper to cut measuring strips

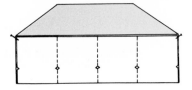

We're using the cake pictured at right as an example. Smoothly ice the cake and let the icing set until a crust forms. It's a good idea to measure and mark a cake before you transfer it from turn table to serving tray or cake board. Then it's all set to decorate. Cut a strip of paper the height of the cake (in this case, 4″) and exactly as long as one side.

There are four scallops on both top and base of this cake, so fold your paper strip into fourths. First fold in half, then fold each half in half, fan fashion. The base scallops start about 2″ up from the bottom, so cut a notch on both sides of the folded strip at that point. Open the strip and pin against cake side. (Corsage pins are handy for this.) Mark the position of the notches and divisions on the side and top edge of the cake with a toothpick. Repeat for other three sides.

Measuring the side of a round cake

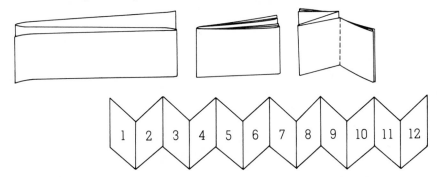

This is almost as easy as measuring a square cake. We're using the cake shown on page 44 to explain the procedure. Cut a strip of paper the width of the height of the cake (about 4″) and just long enough so edges butt when you wrap the strip around the cake. The division here is in twelfths. First fold the strip into thirds, sliding the strip back and forth between your fingers until the divisions are perfectly even. Now fold each third into fourths fan fashion. Crease sharply in fan fashion then open the strip—the creases divide the strip into even twelfths.

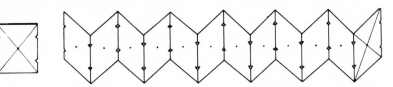

It's essential to mark a round cake before piping bold borders

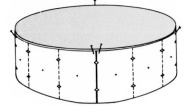

Re-fold the strip to cut notches to position the design of the side border. Find the center by lightly drawing diagonal lines from opposite corners. Make a hole with a pin where lines intersect. This will be the place where the center rosette is piped. Cut notches on both sides of the strip where border design ends at top and bottom, about 1″ from edges.

Open the strip, smooth lightly around cake side and pin. Mark the center holes and notches on the cake with toothpick. Also mark the top edge of the cake at the folds. The cake side is ready to decorate.

How to measure and mark a square cake top

Use the cake above as an example. First cut a parchment or wax paper square with the sides the exact length of the side pattern shown on page 42. Fold the square in half, then in quarters, just like a handkerchief. Open it up and fold again on the diagonal into a triangle. Open again and fold diagonally, matching corners not folded before.

Re-fold on all creases. Measure 2″ down from the center point of the folded square on both sides and cut a gentle curve from mark to mark. Open the square and use the side pattern to make marks midway from center to corner of edges. Connect these marks diagonally across square. Now you have a pattern of a circle with rays extending. Smooth pattern and pin on cake. Mark the edge of the circle with closely spaced pin pricks in the icing. Prick through the paper to mark the rays extending from circle.

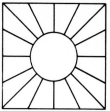

Folding a square of paper makes a pattern for a cake top

Decorate a cheerful sun cake

1. Bake, fill and ice two 8″ square layers, each layer 2″ high. Measure and mark the sides and the top just as described above.

2. Use tube 19 to pipe a shell border at base of cake. Now drop tube 16 string from mark to mark and finish with rosettes. Pipe a curve of tube 13 stars above string. Drop tube 16 string from top edge of cake following marks, then pipe tube 19 upright shells and tube 16 stars.

3. Fill in the circle on top of the cake with closely spaced tube 16 stars. Pipe over the radiating lines with tube 16 shells, then add a rosette with the same tube where the lines meet the string drapes. Complete top border with tube 16 shells. Pipe orange shells around circle with tube 19 and do the features with tube 19 also. Your sunny cake serves twelve.

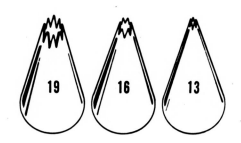

Use your measuring skills on this festive round cake

Isn't this a beautiful example of how only borders can create an impressive cake? The sculptural trim, done with only one star tube, is accented by a delicate use of color. To decorate a cake like this, it's essential to measure and mark not only the side, but the top of the cake too, so all the piping is precisely and evenly spaced.

Mark the iced cake before starting to decorate

Ice the cake, let icing set until it forms a crust, then measure and mark. It's usually best to do this while the cake is still on the turntable—then when you transfer it to a serving tray it's ready to decorate. First measure and mark the side, just as shown on page 42.

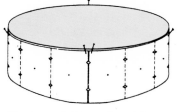

First mark the cake side

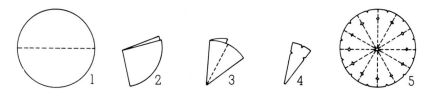

How to mark a round cake top

This is a 10" cake, so first cut a circle 10" in diameter from parchment or wax paper. The easiest way to do this is to trace a 10" cake circle. Fold the circle into halves, then into quarters. Open the circle and fold each quarter into thirds, since we are using a division of twelve. Now refold the circle in fan fashion and crease sharply. From outer cut edge, measure in 1½" and cut a notch on both sides of the fan. Make a tiny cut at the pointed tip of the fan. Cut a notch on the curved edge of fan midway between two folded sides.

Open the circle and gently smooth it over cake top. Line up the folds with the center marks on side of cake. Pin in place. With a toothpick, mark all notches and cake-top center. Remove pattern, set cake on serving tray and you're ready to decorate.

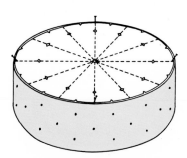

Line up cake-top pattern with marks on side

Only one tube decorates the cake

1. Fill and ice a 10" round, two-layer cake, each layer about 2" high, with buttercream. Mark top and sides as directed above and on page 42. Transfer cake to serving tray. For speed in decorating, pipe almost all the white trim first, then go back and add color accents. Use tube 17 for all trim. Pipe a puffy shell border around base of cake.

2. Pipe the side motifs. Using marks as guides, pipe deeply curved shells, tails extending, to form a series of diamond shapes around side. Where diamonds join in center of cake side, pipe a fleur-de-lis above, and one under mark. Finish each fleur-de-lis with a puffy shell. Your side border is almost complete!

3. Do the top trim. Pipe elongated curved shells from marks within cake top to marked edge of cake. This will form a triangle design with curves of shells touching. Pipe a shell border around edge of cake, leaving a small space where tails of elongated shells join at edge.

4. Finish the trim with tinted icing, using tube 17 again. Frame the shells at the base of cake with curves of icing. Pipe rosettes on side of cake to connect the fleurs-de-lis. Pipe more rosettes in the spaces on top edge of cake. In the center of the cake top, pipe a circle of twelve shells, tails touching, to form a flower. The finishing touch is a white rosette in the middle of the flower. Measuring has made this intricate-looking cake very quick to decorate! Serves 14.

Just one tube does all the trim

Measure and mark before piping these borders on a cake

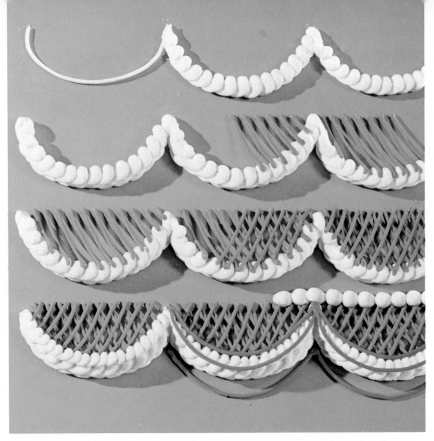

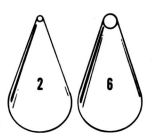

Combine garlands, lattice and string for an outstanding top border

Airy lattice is featured in this showy border for top edge of cake.

1. Drop a series of tube 2 strings as a guide for piping the garlands. Pipe a tube 6 garland with back-and-forth movements.

2. Pipe a second garland on top of the first. Now pipe lattice. Starting in the center of the curve, drop diagonal lines of tube 2 string. Go to the end of the curve, then go back and fill in the other side.

3. Starting again in the center, drop strings in opposing direction. Continue as before until space is filled.

4. To conceal the rough ends of the lattice, use tube 2 and a back-and-forth movement. Drop two rows of tube 2 strings on top of the garland. Add a third string below the garland. Finish the top edge with tube 6 bulbs, piped just like a shell.

To put this border on a round cake, first measure and mark the top edge as described on page 45. A 12″ cake or tier would need twelve divisions.

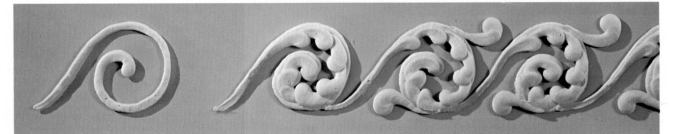

Here's a beautiful scroll border that's a classic favorite for trimming a cake side. Practice it on a propped-up cookie sheet. Tube 6 does all the work. First pipe a curve like a question mark lying on its side. Now go back to the innermost curve and over-pipe with curved shell shapes, blending the tails smoothly into the original curve. Add extensions of curved shells above and below the main curves for a baroque effect. After you've piped this border with round tube 6, try doing it with star tube 19. You'll find it's just as effective. The side of a 10″ cake or tier should be divided into twelfths for this border.

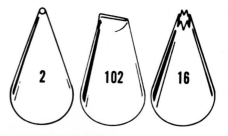

To pipe this fancy border, first drop evenly-spaced tube 2 string guidelines. Spatula stripe a decorating cone fitted with tube 102 with deep pink icing, then fill with lighter pink icing. Hold cone with wide end touching surface, narrow end flaring out, and move hand up and down as you follow the guideline. Above the ruffle, pipe a garland with zigzag motions of tube 16. Thin the icing to pipe the string work. Drop a tube 2 string above the garland and two strings over it. Drop a fourth string below the ruffle. Finish with double loops and little twirls of icing. To put this border on a 12″ cake, divide the top edge into twelfths.

To put a graceful holly vine on a 10′ round cake, first divide cake side into twelfths and mark the depth of the curve as well. Use thinned icing for vine and leaves. Pipe the vine with tube 2 as shown on page 34, and add short strokes for stems of leaves. Now pipe the leaves at the ends of the stems with tube 65. Hold cone at a 45° angle to the surface, squeeze, relax pressure as you move off, stop pressure and draw leaf to a point. After you've piped a few leaves, use a damp artist's brush to pull out the characteristic points. Pipe the holly berries with tube 3. Hold cone straight out from surface and use the method described on page 35.

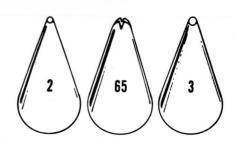

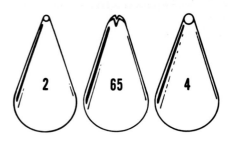

This graceful grape vine is a very traditional cake-side trim. Start by piping a curving vine, just as for the holly vine above. Brush-stripe a cone fitted with tube 2 with brown color from the jar, and fill with thinned green icing. Pull out short stems for leaves, then pipe the rippled leaves with tube 65, keeping them evenly spaced. Use violet icing and tube 4 for the grape clusters, one within each curve. Start at the tip of the cluster and pipe a tear drop, exactly as you would a shell. (See page 33.) Move up the cluster, piping more grapes and massing them in the center. Work quickly and rhythmically. Pipe curly tendrils with tube 2.

Round tubes pipe clear precise borders

Aren't the three cakes above as pretty as a bouquet? Their only trim is borders, all piped with plain round tubes. Cakes done with round tubes require careful pressure control, and neat execution, but the jewel-like results are well worth the care taken in decorating. Measuring and marking are also needed so trim can be evenly spaced.

Round tubes give a lacy look to a petite square

This dainty little confection was planned for a baby shower, but by changing the message and the color scheme, it would be appropriate for many other occasions.

1. Bake a two-layer 8″ square cake, each layer about 2″ high. Chill, fill and ice smoothly with buttercream. Mark a 4″ circle in the center of the cake top. Page 43 shows how to do this with the folded paper method, but you can do it more quickly by using a 4″ round cookie cutter. From the center of each side of the cake edge, make a mark 2″ in with a toothpick. Gently press the cutter within these four marks. Transfer the pattern from the Appendix, starting on page 162, to each cake side. Place cake on serving tray.

2. First write the script message in the center of the marked circle with tube 2 and thinned icing. Page 138 explains the technique. Pipe a neat tube 6 ball border at base of cake. (See page 35.)

3. The delicate, veil-like trim that covers the top of the cake and drapes over the side is known as cornelli lace, and is really very easy to do. It softens the edges of the cake and makes a top border unnecessary. Cornelli looks its best when done against icing of a contrasting color, as here. Use thinned icing and tube 1. Starting at edge of marked circle, holding tube straight out, pipe a trail of curving lines, close together and never touching. Keep an even light pressure and cover as much area as possible without lifting tube. Completely fill the area, down to the marked pattern on cake sides. The closer the lines, the daintier the effect. When cornelli is piped, frame the circle and outline the marked side pattern with tube 2 beading—a series of tiny dots just as you would do a ball border.

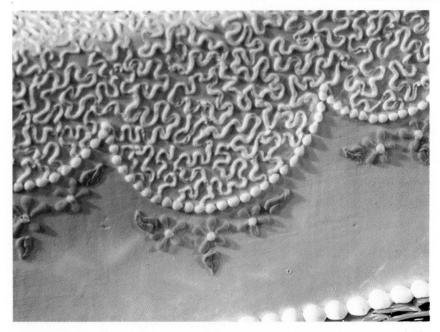

4. Finish the cake with trios of "embroidered" flowers. Pipe teardrop petals with shell technique and tube 1. Add tube 1 dots for centers. Trim with tube 2 leaves, two tiny shell shapes joined. Serve this centerpiece cake to twelve party guests.

Please turn the page for descriptions of the other two cakes on page 48

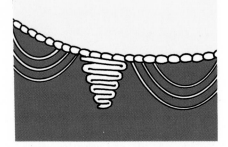

*Pipe the grapes on a
tube 4 zigzag base
to give a rounded effect*

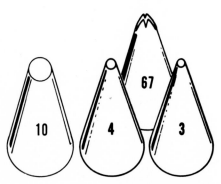

*Tubes 10, 4 and 3
pipe borders, strings and grapes,
tube 67 forms leaves*

Round tubes pipe clusters of luscious grapes

The special magic of round tubes and warmly tinted icing produce a stunning cake to celebrate Thanksgiving. Measure and mark the cake side carefully for neat placement of grapes and string trim.

1. Bake two 10″ round layers, each about 2″ high. Chill, fill, and ice smoothly, side in chocolate, top in white buttercream. Let icing set, then divide side into sixths, using technique on page 42. Fold paper strip in half, then fold each half into thirds. Make a mark on either side of original marks, about ½″ away, to indicate where strings begin. On top of cake, toward the rear, mark freehand the position of three grape clusters, each about 2″ long. Transfer cake to serving tray.

2. Use tube 10 for bottom ball border. Overpipe each ball with a "c" curve done with tube 3 and contrasting icing. Drop tube 3 strings from top edge of cake, first the deepest string from inner marks, then two more strings within it. Pipe script on cake top with tube 3 and the technique shown on page 138. Finish the top edge with a tube 4 ball border.

3. Pipe the grape clusters. These are done in a similar way to the grape clusters on page 47, but the rounded effect is achieved by piping the grapes on a base of icing. Use tube 4 and rose tinted icing to pipe tight zigzags to form triangles on the side of the cake between the strings. See diagram at left. Now go back and cover the zigzag triangles with grapes. Start just below the point of the triangle and pipe shell shapes to cover completely the piped base.

When the side clusters are piped, pipe three more on top of cake. First pipe three zigzag triangular bases, then cover with shells, working from tip to top of triangle.

4. Finish the cake with tube 67 leaves at the top of the grape clusters. Use thinned icing and pull them out to perky points. A holiday masterpiece that serves 14 guests.

Round tubes make beautiful formal borders

This rosy, feminine cake is adorned only with precisely piped borders, trimmed and built up for a baroque, dimensional effect. All are achieved with basic forms done with plain round tubes. Decorate it for any important occasion, varying the message and color as you desire.

1. Bake, chill and fill a two-layer, 9" or 10" round cake, each layer about 2" high. Ice smoothly, let icing crust, then measure and mark.

Divide cake side into twelfths, using method shown on page 42. Mark each division on top edge of cake. On top of cake, mark scallops, about 1" at deepest point, from mark to mark. Do this freehand, or more quickly by gently pressing a 2½" round cookie cutter into the icing. Transfer cake to serving tray or cake board.

2. Write script message in center of cake top with tube 2, as shown on page 138. Pipe a tube 10 ball border at base of cake, then drop tube 2 string around each ball, topping the points with dots. Drop a string guideline for garlands from mark to mark of top edge of cake. Pipe the garlands over the guidelines with tube 10. Using a quick back-and-forth movement, start with light pressure. Increase pressure and lift tube to let garland build up at center, then decrease pressure to finish curve. Drop tube 2 strings above garlands, then over and below them. Use tube 2 again to pipe scalloped edging below garlands. Pipe an upright, inverted shell shape with tube 6 between each garland. Add tube 2 dots.

3. Use tube 10 to pipe garlands on marked scallops on top of cake. Drop a tube 2 string over each garland and outline each with a second string. Do hearts between garlands by piping two tube 6 shell shapes, sides touching. Pipe a tube 6 bulb border on top edge of cake, using shell technique. Serve this ornate creation to twelve.

Three plain round tubes pipe the classic borders

You'll use variations of these borders many times on original cakes you design yourself

CHAPTER FIVE   # A cake can make a party!

Here's a portfolio of striking cakes arranged by season to set the theme and be the centerpiece of any celebration from New Year's Eve all through the year to Christmas day.

Browse through this chapter to see a flowery horseshoe cake to wish good luck for the coming year, heart-shaped love cakes for Valentine's day and a sparkly winter snowflake cake. There are personality cakes to give joy to children and the young in heart and a bunny in a basket for Easter fun. View garden-y cakes for summer, harvest cakes for fall and cookie-trimmed treats for Christmas.

A beautiful party cake can brighten any day of the year! So after you've mastered the basic techniques in this book, get out your tubes and mix some icing—create some holiday masterpieces of your own.

Flowers are always in season

Here's a spectacular tray of just-like-real flowers to bring to a church box supper, present to a hostess, or center the table at a special luncheon or dinner. Each is piped with large tubes and placed on a cupcake.

First review the flower making techniques—page 97 for wild roses, violets and daisies, page 100 for the pansy and page 101 for the rose. The techniques for these flowers will be just the same—but even easier because the blossoms are bigger.

1. First pipe the flowers in buttercream. Use a large number 13 flower nail for all. Tube 127 does the daisy, pansy and rose. For a subtly pretty rose, spatula-stripe the cone with pink icing, then fill with yellow. Add a yellow center to the daisy with tube 6, to the pansy with tube 4. Wild flowers and violets are piped with tube 104 with tube 4 stamens. Pipe violet leaves just like a rounded petal with tube 104.

Here's how to create the giant daffodil. Pipe five petals on the number 13 nail with tube 127, just like the wild rose. Dip your fingers in cornstarch and pinch the tips of the petals for a pointed look. In the center of the flower, coil a tube 4 spiral into a cup shape. Edge with tube 4 dots. (For a regular-size flower, use tubes 104 and 3.)

Freeze all the flowers and the violet leaves.

2. Bake a batch of cupcakes, swirl the tops with buttercream and edge with tube 13 shells. Pipe a little mound of icing on the center of each and gently press on the frozen flowers. Position violet leaves before adding flowers. Trim all the other flowers with tube 70 leaves. The frozen flowers will thaw in just a few moments. Arrange the cupcake flowers on a tray and wait for applause!

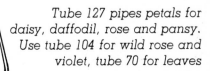

Tube 127 pipes petals for daisy, daffodil, rose and pansy. Use tube 104 for wild rose and violet, tube 70 for leaves

Wish good luck for the year to come

Here's a horseshoe-shaped cake heaped with bright flowers and crossed by a banner bearing your greetings. Use it as the centerpiece for a New Year's Eve supper, or a New Year's Day buffet.

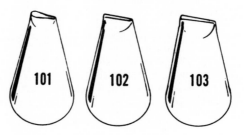

Use rose tubes for the flowers

Pipe the flowers first

We used roses, daisies and wild roses piped with tubes 101, 102 and 103. (See Chapter 6, starting page 92.) Make them from buttercream and freeze, or use royal icing and air-dry. If you've saved flowers from practice sessions, this is an ideal cake to use them on. Go through your store and choose the colors that harmonize. Royal icing flowers will soften somewhat as they rest on the buttercream-covered cake. Frozen buttercream flowers will thaw in just a few moments.

Prepare the ribbon banner

Notch the ends of a 14" length of satin ribbon, 2" wide. Using the ribbon as pattern, cut a "lining" of wax paper. Secure the ribbon to the wax paper strip with tiny dots of royal icing. Pin the lined ribbon to a piece of corrugated cardboard and pipe the message with tube 2. Use a mixture of half royal icing, half piping gel.

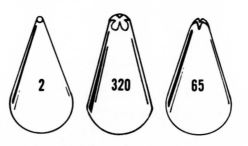

Tube 2 for the script,
a star tube for border,
tube 65 for leaves

Decorate the cake

Bake a cake in an 11" horseshoe pan, chill and ice smoothly with buttercream. Use the pan as a pattern to cut a base from corrugated cardboard and cover with foil. Set cake on base.

Pipe the interesting reverse shell border with tube 320—or you may prefer to use tube 19.

Now for the fun of putting it all together! Lay the ribbon banner diagonally across the cake. Now cover the cake top with flowers. Pipe a dot of icing on the back of each to attach. Finish the cake with tube 65 leaves piped with thinned buttercream. This 11" good luck cake serves twelve merry-makers.

Valentine's Day gives us an opportunity to express our feelings to those we love—and decorating a cake with hearts, flowers, ruffles and roses is such a sweet way to do it. So break the dreary routine of winter days—plan a party to celebrate love!

A flowery Valentine cake

Here's a pretty heart-shaped cake to decorate for your love that says it all with flowers.

1. Pipe the wild roses in advance in royal icing. Review page 97 for technique. Use tubes 101 and 102 for two sizes of petals and finish with tube 1 stamens.

2. Bake, chill and fill a two-layer 9" heart cake. Ice in buttercream and place on cake board or tray. Pipe tube 21 stars at base and frame each star with tube 101s. Do top shell border with tube 19, then add the fluted ribbon with tube 104. Attach the flowers with dots of icing, then pipe tube 65 leaves with thinned buttercream. This pretty treat serves twelve.

A double-heart Valentine cake

Two hearts entwined make a very sweet surprise for your valentine.

1. Make lots of roses and buds with royal icing and tubes 101 and 102. Set aside to dry. See page 101 for technique.

2. Bake, chill and fill two cakes in 9" heart pans, each cake two layers. Ice one cake in pink buttercream, the other in white. Make a pattern by tracing the heart pan twice and cutting out the shapes. Overlap the two hearts, tape in place, and mark the pink cake where the white cake curves into it. Trim this curve off the pink cake. Use the same pattern to cut a cake base from corrugated cardboard, adding 1" all around. Cover with foil and fit cakes together on it. Transfer arrow pattern to cake top. (Appendix, starting page 162.)

3. Use tube 16 for most trim. Outline the arrow with tight zigzags. Pipe a shell border at base, then curved zigzag garlands above it. Border hearts at top edge with shells, then pipe a second row of shells beneath it, omitting curve where hearts join. Use tube 2 and thinned icing in deep pink to pipe the message, add scallops and dots within top border and over-pipe the arrow. Drop string drapes over the garlands at base of cake. Now add the roses as picture shows, attaching with dots of icing. Trim the flowers with tube 65 leaves. This spectacular tribute serves 20 party guests.

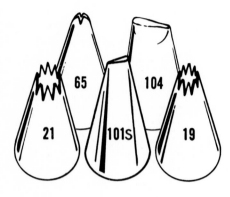

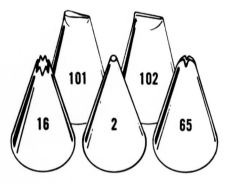

Spell out love on a fluted heart

Here's the same old message said in a bold new way! If your valentine doesn't care for ruffles and roses, decorate this striking showpiece for him. It's simple and tailored, but very sweet!

Make the Color Flow designs in advance

Review page 116 for technique, then tape patterns for large and small hearts to glass, plexiglass or stiff cardboard, tape wax paper over, and do outlining in bright red icing with tube 3. Let outlines dry about an hour, then fill in with thinned icing. Dry about 48 hours.

Decorate the cake

Bake, chill and fill a 9" two-layer heart cake. Ice with buttercream or boiled icing. Use tube 6 to pipe base bulb border, done just like a shell border. Attach small Color Flow hearts to cake side with dots of icing, spacing evenly. Pipe tube 104 curves below hearts, jiggling hand between each curve for a fluted effect. Pipe mounds of icing on cake top and set large Color Flow heart on them. Edge the top of the cake with a tube 104 fluted border, using a back and forth movement. Serve to twelve. Run a knife blade under the large heart and lift off cake before cutting. Save it for a memento of the party.

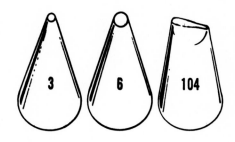

Decorate a sparkling snowflake cake

Use one of nature's most beautiful designs to grace a masterpiece cake. Iced in palest green and trimmed with six-pointed sparkling stars, this is a centerpiece worthy of your nicest dinner party. Serve it on Twelfth Night, or any winter occasion.

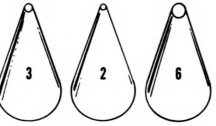

Pipe snowflakes with royal icing. Do borders with tube 6

Make the snowflakes first

These are done off the cake in a technique called over-piping. Tape the pattern for the large snowflake to a piece of stiff cardboard, glass or plastic. Tape wax paper smoothly over it. Trace the pattern with tube 3 and royal icing. Allow to dry for an hour or so, then over-pipe the design with tube 2. Dry again and over-pipe the main lines with tube 2 again. Use a steady, careful hand. As soon as you've finished the final piping, sprinkle the design with edible glitter.

Do the side snowflakes the same way, but tape patterns to a 10" curved form before taping wax paper over. Pipe with tube 3, dry, then over-pipe main lines with tube 2 and sprinkle with glitter. Dry thoroughly. You will need six, but make extras—they're fragile.

Decorate the cake

The cake itself is very simple to set off the sparkling snowflakes. Bake, chill and fill a two-layer 10" round cake. Make sure the layers are about 2" high. Ice in buttercream, let icing crust, then divide the side into sixths (see page 42) and mark in center of side. Set cake on serving tray.

Pipe plain ball borders using tube 6.

Attach the snowflakes

Remove the piped snowflakes from wax paper. For large snowflake, trim taped edges of paper with a sharp knife. Place a piece of soft foam over snowflake, then a piece of stiff cardboard. Turn over this "sandwich" and lift off cardboard. Design will be upside down. Peel off paper. Carefully place snowflake in center of cake.

For small snowflakes, trim taped wax paper edges, turn over curved form and let snowflake rest in your palm. Peel off paper, pipe a few dots of icing on back of snowflake and gently press to side of cake, using marks as guide for placement.

This winter masterpiece serves 14.

OLD KING COLE

Old King Cole
Was a merry old soul,
And a merry old soul was he;
He called for his pipe,
And he called for his bowl,
And he called for his fiddlers three.

MISTRESS MARY

Mistress Mary, quite contrary,
How does your garden grow?
With silver bells and cockle shells
And pretty maids all in a row.

LITTLE MISS MUFFET

Little Miss Muffet
Sat on a tuffet,
Eating some curds and whey;
There came a great spider,
And sat down beside her,
And frightened Miss Muffet away.

Surprise the youngsters with a nursery rhyme cake!

Have an impromptu after-school party! Ask the children to bring friends home, then bring them to the table for glasses of milk and one of these entertaining cakes. Their eyes will sparkle! For a really big party, decorate all three—they'll steal the show!

All of the cakes start the same. Bake in a Wonder Mold pan, set on cake circle cut to size, and ice with flesh-colored buttercream. Then have fun bringing the character to life.

Old King Cole has a genial disposition

For a regal touch, set the cake on a board edged with a gilt cake ruffle. Pipe strands of hair and mustache with tube 32. Use tube 10 to pipe the blue eyes, then flatten with a fingertip. Pipe pink cheeks the same way and flatten. Use tube 10 again to pipe balls for nose and mouth. Set a plastic make-believe crown on his head, or make one from gold-color cardboard. King Cole is dressed for the party! Serves twelve.

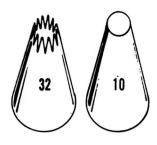

Mary refuses to cheer up

To indicate this little girl's garden, pipe royal icing daisies with tube 103, add tube 3 centers and dry in a curved form (See page 97.)

In addition to the Wonder Mold cake, bake a 10" round layer. Ice grass green, set on cake board and edge with tube 32 shells. Press a cake circle on top of layer to mark an 8" circle. To support Wonder Mold cake, insert six ¼" dowels within circle and clip off level with top. See page 146 for method. Center Wonder Mold cake on cake layer.

Pipe a fluted ruffle with tube 104 around Mary's neck, using a back and forth motion. Pipe her chocolate brown hair with tube 32 and use tube 10 to pipe eyes and cheeks, just as for King Cole. Do the down-curved mouth with tube 3. Attach daisies to base cake and hair-do with dots of icing. Secure glittered plastic bells to edge of base cake with pieces of toothpick. Trim flowers and bells with tube 65 leaves. Serves 18.

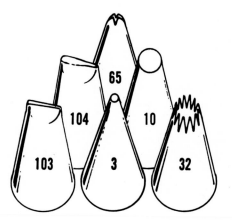

Little Miss Muffet is alarmed

The spider who is the cause of her fright is really harmless. Twist three 1½" lengths of fine wire together in center and bend ends of wire for six legs. Pipe an oval in center for spider's body with black royal icing. Ice a cupcake for Miss Muffet's hat.

Set Wonder Mold cake on a foil-covered 10" cake board and add a feminine touch by pushing in a dainty blue cake ruffle. Pipe strokes of yellow icing for hair with tube 32, ending about halfway down side. Do the sausage curls with curves piped with the same tube. Pipe cheeks and nose with tube 10 the same as for King Cole. Outline oval mouth with tube 4 and brush in thinned icing. Pipe white tube 10 balls for eyes, flatten with a fingertip then top with tube 4 blue balls and flatten again. Add tube 4 chocolate brown lashes.

Gather a 12" length of cake ruffle for hat brim. Attach to top of head with dots of icing, then pipe a mound of icing and set cupcake on it. Trim hat with a tube 46 ribbon, then set your handmade spider on it. No wonder Miss Muffet is afraid! Serves twelve.

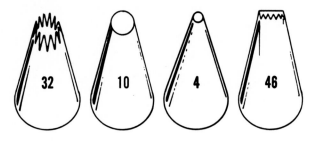

Pipe the sweet peas
with a "rose" tube

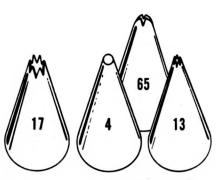

Do fluffy borders
in pink buttercream

Pipe the flowers in advance

Sweet peas in clusters and cascades give a ruffly feminine look to a cake, and they're very quick and easy to do. Use royal icing, tube 103 and the directions on page 96 to pipe many of them. Dry thoroughly.

Decorate the cake

This little cake takes just one mix, but the sparkling clear pillars that elevate the tiers make it look just as impressive as a wedding cake. Your little girl will be thrilled when she sees it.

1. Bake and chill three single-layer cake tiers using 5", 7½" and 9" Mini-tier pans. Ice with buttercream. Trace 9" pan on corrugated cardboard, cut board 1" larger all around and cover with foil. Set 9" tier on board and push the sewn edge of a cake ruffle under it with a small knife. Set 5" and 7½" tiers on corresponding Mini-tier separator plates. Insert legs from separator set in projections on underside of 8" plate and carefully center over base tier. Gently push legs into base tier until they touch cake board. Assemble top tier the same way.

2. Pipe a tube 17 reverse shell border at base of bottom tier. Mark heart shapes freehand on side of tier and pipe with tube 4 and "e" motion. Add a top shell border with tube 13.

3. All three tiers are decorated with the same tubes. Pipe tube 17 stars at base of middle tier. Mark heart shapes on side of tier and pipe with tube 4 and "e" motion. Using separator legs as guide, mark a heart about 1" in from edge on top of tier. Pipe with tube 13 reverse shells, then pipe a shell border on edge of tier with the same tube.

Do base star border on top tier with tube 17, top shell border with tube 13.

4. Finish the two lower tiers with sweet peas in clusters and cascades, attaching with dots of icing. Pipe a heavy curve of icing on top tier and press in flowers. Trim all flowers with tube 65 leaves. This frilly little centerpiece serves twelve—cut two slices from the top tier, four from the middle tier and six from the base tier.

Party
plans

Make everything rosy at the party

Spread the table with a pink cloth and set the marvelous cake in the center. Serve creamed chicken flecked with red pimento in heart-shaped pastry cases, cinnamon apples and a fruit salad molded in red gelatin. Dessert is delicious—strawberry sundaes to eat with the cake! For a festive touch, top each with a pretty Valentine pick. Make a bowl of red fruit punch, and freeze some of it in the 5" heart pan to float on top. A garnish of cherries and mint leaves is pretty.

Little girls love surprises, so fill a lacy plastic heart box with an inexpensive chain or bracelet for each guest. They'll never forget this festive "grown-up" celebration—and wasn't it worth it to take the trouble for little extra touches!

Would you like to make a
little girl very happy?
Plan a Valentine party
      and center the table
with this rosy tier cake

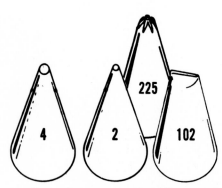

Cupcakes, a marshmallow and just a little decorating make a jolly snow person

Happy snow people greet the children

After a day of skating or sledding down snowy slopes, the children will be delighted by these cupcake snow people, gaily dressed in mittens and mufflers. Bring them out with mugs of hot chocolate topped with whipped cream.

1. Use your favorite recipe or mix to bake cupcakes in small and medium sizes. Chill, then cover thickly with boiled icing. The easy way to do this is to spear a fork into the bottom of the cupcake, then swirl on the icing. The heads are marshmallows. Spear each with a toothpick, then cover with icing.

Let icing set a little, then stack a medium and small cupcake for body. Insert a toothpicked marshmallow on top.

2. The snow lady wears a flowery bonnet! Figure pipe the arms with tube 4 and boiled icing and use the same tube for the red mittens. (See Chapter Eight, page 109 for method.) Pipe a smile and eyes with tube 2 and press in a piece of corn candy for nose. Do bonnet strings and bow with tube 102, then attach made-ahead tube 225 drop flowers with dots of icing to form the bonnet. Finish her costume with tube 2 buttons.

3. The snow men are decorated in a similar fashion. Figure pipe arms and mittens with tube 4, do features and buttons with tube 2 and tie tube 102 mufflers around their necks. For a debonair touch, we gave each a plastic top hat with a bright tube 102 band and added a plastic cane.

1. First review page 116 for method, then make the Color Flow trims. Patterns are in Appendix, starting page 162. Tape pattern for top design to stiff cardboard, glass or plexiglass and cover with wax paper. Outline with tube 2, then thin icing and tint in three shades of pink. Fill in design and dry 48 hours.

2. You will need eight curved side pieces. Tape pattern to a 12" curved form and tape wax paper smoothly over it. The form will hold three or four patterns. Outline entire patterns, then prop up form on crumpled foil so right side is relatively level, and fill in heart and flowers on right side of design *only*. Dry, then prop form again so left side is level and fill in heart and flower on left side of design. If you attempt to fill in entire design at once, the curve of the form may cause the thinned fill-in icing to run over the outlines.

3. Bake and chill a 12" two-layer round tier and a single-layer 9" heart tier. Fill, then ice the round tier—white on side, pink on top. Divide into eighths and mark on center of side with a toothpick. (See page 42.) Place on serving tray or cake board. Ice the heart tier white and set on round tier, slightly to the rear. Use tube 10 to pipe ball borders on round tier, tube 8 to border the top tier.

Peel wax paper off Color Flow designs. Pipe mounds of icing on back of top design and place on cake. Pipe mounds of icing on backs of curved designs and carefully press to side of base tier, using marks as guides. This Valentine present serves 28. Before serving, run a knife under the Color Flow designs and lift off.

Hearts and flowers send a message of love

Round tubes pipe the borders

Everybody's Irish on March 17... so plan a party to please your Irish friends and set the theme with one of these Gaelic cakes. Corned beef and cabbage is the time-honored entree, but Irish stew will do fine too. Green dress required.

Jewel-like shamrocks grace a tier cake

Glittering hard candy hearts form shamrocks. Once you've made hard candy, you'll think of lots of ways to use it for cake trims.

1. Brush heart molds for hard candy with oil, then make the candy.

HARD CANDY RECIPE

2 cups granulated sugar
2/3 cup water
¼ teaspoon cream of tartar

2 drops peppermint extract
2 or 3 drops liquid food coloring

Combine water, sugar and cream of tartar in a three-quart saucepan and bring to boil, stirring constantly. Now stir in coloring, insert candy thermometer and stop stirring. Continue cooking over high heat, occasionally brushing sides of pan and thermometer with a wet pastry brush to prevent crystals from forming. At 280°F, turn to low heat and stir in flavoring. At 300°F, remove from heat and pour into molds. Chill until hard, then pop out of molds.

2. Bake and chill a single-layer oval tier and a 9" x 13" sheet cake, about 3" high. Ice both tiers smoothly with boiled icing and assemble on a cake board. Edge both tiers with tube 5 bulbs.

3. On oval tier, use green-tinted piping gel and tube 1 to pipe a spray of stems. Do tiny shamrocks by piping heart shapes, two shells with sides touching. Arrange hard candy hearts in groups of three for large shamrocks. Pipe stems and shamrocks on side of base tier and attach candy hearts on mounds of icing. Add a blue piping gel bow and write message with tube 1. This shining centerpiece serves 18.

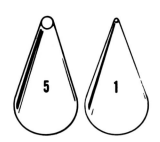

Two tubes finish the simple cake

Invite a loveable leprechaun to the party

1. Bake a cake in a rag doll pan, chill, then trim off long curls and ice to top of head for hat. Prepare a corrugated cardboard cake base by tracing pan, then cover with green foil. Set cake on board.

2. Quick-to-pipe stars cover most of the cake. First ice cake thinly with buttercream, then outline all color areas with tube 3. Fill in areas with tube 16 stars, set close together. Pipe a row of zigzags at boot tops. Starting at bottom, pull out short tube 16 strands for tousled hair. Pipe a line of icing with tube 21 for hat brim, then pipe a second line on top of it.

3. Pipe cheeks and eyes with tube 10, then flatten with your fingertip. Pipe pink nose with same tube. Use tube 3 for mouth, bow and buttons. For shamrock trim on boots, pipe heart shapes, two shells touching, with tube 3. To make the pipe, insert a short length of a plastic drinking straw into a marshmallow. Ice chocolate, then cover side of marshmallow with tube 16 stars. Serve to twelve.

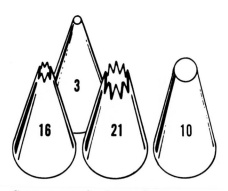

Stars cover the leprechaun

On these two pages are cakes that owe their appeal to unusual shapes and the star technique. You'll be delighted at the versatility and ease of this method. First the cake is thinly iced in buttercream just as you would for a crumb coating. Clear precise areas of color are assured by first outlining the areas, then filling in with quick stars. This gives a pleasing, velvety texture to the surface. Buttercream in regular consistency is best for this work.

Two happy faces decorate anniversary cakes

The cakes for this quaint couple were surprisingly baked in bell-shaped pans. Study the Mr. and Mrs. patterns in the Appendix, starting page 162, then adapt them to resemble the hair styles and clothing the couple wore at the time of their wedding.

1. Bake and chill two single-layer cakes in 9" bell pans. Ice the sides of one cake smoothly in pink and stroke a thin coat of icing on top of cake. Ice the second cake in yellow. Transfer patterns to cake tops by pricking through with a pin. Set first cake on tray and border with tube 10 shell-motion bulbs. Set second cake on tray and pipe border with same tube.

2. Outline all color areas with tube 3, and flesh-color icing. Pipe an outline around edges of cakes too. Now mix up tinted icing and fill areas with tube 16 stars, setting them close together and holding tube straight up, perpendicular to surface.

3. On "Mrs." cake, pipe ruffle trim with tube 104, wide end of tube touching surface, narrow end flaring out. Use a back and forth movement. Add buttons and eyes with tube 10. Use tube 10 again to pipe eyes on "Mr." cake. The couple is complete and will serve twelve.

Would you like a larger cake to serve a crowd? Bake a 12" x 18" sheet cake, ice and edge with bulb borders, then set the Mr. and Mrs. cakes on it. A single-layer sheet cake, 12" x 18", will serve 27.

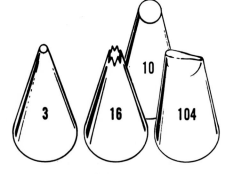

To bring back memories, serve the same menu that was served at the couple's bridal reception. And ask the guests to wear outfits in the style of the wedding year. You'll be surprised at how funny those mini-skirts look!

A baby doll cake for a baby shower

This cute little cake is shaped like a baby and "dressed" in a frock as pretty as a christening gown. Invite friends to a party to honor the mother-to-be. Serve a light luncheon of crêpes or a quiche, a fresh garden salad and this sweet cake for dessert. And plan on lots of time to linger over coffee and exclaim over the daintily wrapped gifts!

1. Make tiny pink roses in advance in royal icing and tube 101s. Follow the directions on page 101. Dry thoroughly.

2. Bake and chill a cake in a rag doll pan. Cut off curl area above doll's shoulders and ice to skirt to give a flared look. Cover entire cake thinly with white buttercream, then use a toothpick to indicate tops of booties, edge of hem and sleeves, neckline and front placket trim. Using marks as guides, outline with tube 3. Place cake on serving tray.

3. Use tube 16 for all star fill-in. Pipe flesh-colored arms, legs and face first, extending stars to cover entire head. Use tube 104 and a back and forth movement to pipe white ruffles above booties and at hemline down to cake plate. Change to tube 102 to pipe hemline ruffles on cake plate and ruffles that edge sleeves. Add tube 3 pink beading above ruffles as picture shows.

Now fill in booties and dress area up to placket with tube 16 white stars. Go back and pipe stars over sleeves a second time for a puffed effect. Pipe a ruffle around placket with tube 102, edge with tube 3 pink beading, then fill in placket with stars. Add tube 3 buttons and tie "figure 8" bows on sleeves and booties with same tube.

4. Pipe cheeks and eyes with tube 10 balls and flatten with a finger tip. Pipe a tube 10 ball for nose and a tube 3 heart-shaped mouth. The golden curls are piped with tube 3 in tiny "c" curves. Finish the dainty dress by attaching roses on dots of icing. This appealing treat serves twelve.

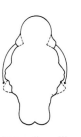

Trim "curl" areas from cake and use for skirt flare

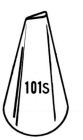

Pipe roses ahead with tube 101s

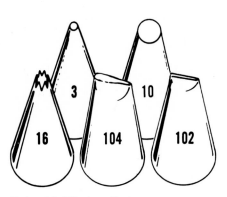

Tube 16 fills in all stars, petal and round tubes add details

Decorate an Easter tableau

Showers and flowers and fresh green leaves show that spring is here—it's time for the Easter Bunny to make his welcome appearance. Decorate this enchanting centerpiece for the Easter table. With scoops of fruit-flavored ice cream it will serve as dessert as well. There's never been a more delightful Easter cake!

Taken in steps, this extravaganza is quite easy to do. The sugar eggs can be molded well in advance and the baking can be done even weeks ahead of time, too, and the cakes frozen until you're ready to decorate.

First prepare the Easter eggs

1. Before starting, review the sugar molding technique described on page 105. Mix sugar with egg white, then divide into several portions and tint each a different dainty pastel. Keep containers tightly covered. Mold the sugar in 3" egg molds. To reduce the weight of the eggs, hollow them out after they've dried about an hour and a half. Page 107 tells how.

2. When the hollow halves of the eggs are completely dry, put them together with a line of royal icing. Dry again, then tint the icing in varied colors and have fun decorating the eggs.

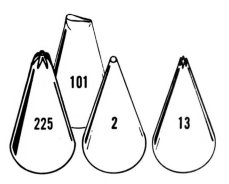

Invent trims with small tubes

Small tubes are used for all trims. Make drop flowers ahead with tube 225 and add tube 2 centers. Cover the seams of the eggs with zigzags or shells with tube 13. Decorate only the top halves of the eggs. Make little bouquets with tube 2 and tie with tube 101 ribbons. Use tube 2 to make scallops and rickrack designs, or just polka-dot the eggs with drop flowers, attaching with dots of icing. Use your own imagination to dream up all kinds of pretty designs.

Decorate the Easter bunny

1. Prepare a cake base by tracing a two-piece bunny mold on stiff corrugated cardboard and covering with clear plastic wrap. Bake a cake in the two-piece mold, using a firm, pound cake recipe. Chill the cake, or cool, wrap closely with plastic wrap and freeze. Fill the two halves of the cake with buttercream and set upright on prepared cake base.

2. Cover the entire bunny with a thin coat of buttercream. Use pink icing and tube 3 to outline the inner area of ears and the eyes. Let outline set, then fill in eyes with thinned icing.

3. Now cover the entire cake with tiny "c" shapes piped with tube 17. Before icing sets, trace nose and mouth with a toothpick and pipe with tube 3 in red icing. Tie a ribbon around his neck and bunny is complete.

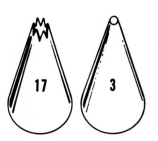

A star tube pipes bunny's fur

Prepare the basket cake

1. A sheet cake serves as the base for this Easter creation. Bake a two-layer 9" x 13" cake and chill or freeze. Fill, then cover cake sides with a thin coat of yellow buttercream. Tint icing green, then cover top thickly and pat with a clean damp sponge for a grassy effect. Set on foil-covered cake board.

2. Review page 142 and do basket weaving with tube 48. Border top edge with curved shells piped with tube 21.

Gently press the closed bunny mold on the cake top to mark position of bunny cake. Insert six or seven ¼" dowels within outline and clip off level with surface to support weight of cake. (See page 146.) Set bunny on basket and surround him with decorated eggs.

The basket serves 24, the bunny slices into twelve pieces, if you can bear to cut him, and the eggs are souvenirs for the children.

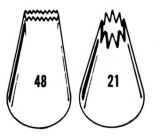

Tube 48 weaves the basket

Outline giraffe with tube 3

Any time is a good time for a children's party, so decorate this irresistible cake, add ice cream and soft drinks and invite the neighborhood youngsters. They'll all adore the loveable, lanky giraffe.

Do the giraffe in Color Flow

Review page 116 for the technique, then tape pattern from Appendix, starting page 162, to a stiff surface, tape wax paper smoothly over and do all outlining with tube 3 and brown icing. Let outlines dry about an hour, then fill in with thinned icing. Dry the giraffe about 48 hours. For needed strength, since the giraffe is so tall, turn over and outline all outer edges again, then fill in with thinned icing. Dry 48 hours.

Bake and decorate the cookies

You will need 14 cookies for trim. Use the recipe on page 18 or your own favorite, and cut out the shapes with a giraffe cookie cutter about 3½" high. After cookies have baked and cooled, paint them with thinned Color Flow icing. Allow to dry, then use Color Flow icing straight from the batch to add the trims. Spots, eyes and smiles are piped with tube 2. Pipe manes with tube 5 and a shell motion. Set aside to dry.

Prepare the long, long cake

Bake the cake in a long loaf pan, 16" x 4" high. Angel food is a good choice for this pan, but any favorite recipe or mix is fine. Don't be timid about color—ice the sides in light orange and the top in bright magenta buttercream. Place on foil-covered cake board cut 1" larger than pan all around. Pipe chocolate bulb borders with tube 6.

Put it all together

Lightly trace the giraffe pattern on top of the cake with a toothpick. Attach flat sugar cubes within the outline on dots of icing. These will support the giraffe. Use half-cubes for narrow areas of feet and tail. Pipe a little mound on the back of each cookie giraffe's head and lean him against the cake side. Carefully peel wax paper off the back of the Color Flow giraffe. Bring the cake to the table and lay the large giraffe on the sugar cubes. After everyone has enjoyed this jolly pet, lift him off to save for another cake, another party. Give each guest a cookie, then slice the cake into 16 neat 1" pieces.

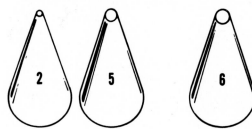

Two tubes trim the cookies　　　*One tube borders the cake*

Set a very tall pet on a long, long cake,

surround him with lots of little pets,

one for each child.

You've made an instant party!

**Light up a tier cake
on Mother's Day**

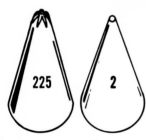

Drop flowers are quick to pipe

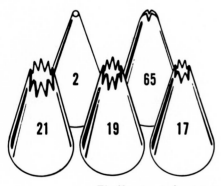

*Fluffy star tube trim
is set off by stringwork*

1. Plan ahead and the decorating will go smoothly. Days, or weeks, before Mother's Day, pipe the rosy flowers with tube 225 and royal icing. Add tube 2 centers and dry. Page 94 shows the quick method.

2. Bake the tiers ahead of time, if you like, and freeze them or bake them two days in advance, wrap well in clear plastic and refrigerate.

Using Mother's favorite recipe, bake a two-layer 12″ tier, each layer about 2″ high and a two-layer 8″ tier, each layer about 1½″ high. Fill and ice each tier with buttercream, then assemble. Insert dowels in 12″ tier to support weight of upper tier. See page 146.

Divide 12″ tier into twelfths, 8″ tier into eighths and mark with a toothpick at top edge. Page 42 shows method. Transfer pattern in Appendix, starting page 162, to top of 8″ tier, or more quickly, press a Pattern Press to top of tier. Design will be clearly imprinted. Make heart pattern for tier sides by folding a piece of paper in two, sketching a half-heart and cutting out. Heart should be about 3″ wide by 3″ high. Using marks as guides, trace four times on upper tier side, six times on lower tier.

3. Pipe a shell border at base of 12″ tier with tube 21 and a top border with tube 19. Outline hearts with curved shells piped with tube 17. Pipe two curved shells in a "V" shape below hearts. Drop parallel triple strings with tube 2 and twirl a little ring at ends of each.

4. On top tier, pipe a tube 19 base border. Outline heart shapes with tube 17 curved shells, then drape tube 2 strings between hearts and finish with rings. Pipe top design with tube 2 and push in candle.

Pipe green stems within all hearts with tube 2, then attach flowers with dots of icing. Cluster more flowers around candle. Finish with tube 65 leaves. This pretty tribute to Mother will serve 32.

Trim a happy cake for Father

Would you like to make Dad very happy on his day? Write him an I.O.U. of chores you'll take over for a week—or a month. Tell him you'll wash the car, mow the lawn, paint the screens and clean the barbecue grill. He'll have more time for golf, tennis or just plain loafing! Then bring out this jolly cake after a big steak dinner. The smile on the icing portrait will match his own broad grin.

1. Bake a 10″ two-layer cake in his favorite flavor. (For most fathers, chocolate.) Chill the layers, then fill with buttercream. Ice the top with white buttercream, the sides chocolate. Transfer pattern from the Appendix, starting page 162, to cake top.

2. The portrait is done with tube 16. Tint buttercream flesh-color, and small amounts rose, red and blue. Use chocolate buttercream for brown areas, untinted for white shirt. Starting with features and necktie, fill in with neat stars, set very close together. Hold cone straight up.

3. Pipe a base border with tubes 21 and 104 just like the one on the bottom of page 36. Do the top shell border with tube 19. Now pipe the tailored string design with tube 2. Drop a curve from the base of one shell and attach below the fifth shell. Go back and drop a string from third shell to fifth shell from it. Continue dropping strings around cake. This gives an interesting overlapping effect, easily done by using the shell border as a spacing guide.

Serve this smiling treat to 14 cheering guests.

Stars pipe the portrait quickly

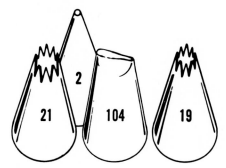

Simple forms with color contrast pipe interesting borders

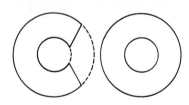

*Trim a wedge from
one cake, then fit together*

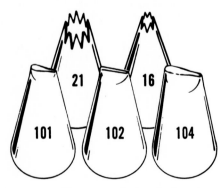

*Roses and simple borders
decorate the cake*

Rings and roses announce an engagement

Bake a cake in the symbolic shape of intertwined rings, cover it with palest pink icing, wreath it with fluffy garlands, then trim with love's own flower. There couldn't be a sweeter cake to honor the bride-to-be!

1. Make the royal icing roses and rosebuds in advance. Tint icing in three shades of pink and pipe them following the directions on page 101. Use tubes 101, 102 and 104 for varied sizes. Set aside to dry.

2. Bake two cakes in 11" ring molds and chill. Trace mold twice on paper, cut out and overlap shapes to determine amount to cut off one cake. Use tracing as pattern to cut out cake base from corrugated cardboard. If you do not have an oval tray large enough to hold cake, use the same pattern to cut a cake board, cutting it 1" larger all around and covering with foil. Set cakes together on cake base and ice in buttercream. Transfer to tray or foil-covered board.

3. Divide curves of cakes into eighths, using your eye as guide. First divide in halves, then fourths, then eighths and mark at top edge with a toothpick. Pipe a tube 21 base shell border. Use tube 16 to pipe fluffy curving garlands from mark to mark in a zigzag motion. Border top edge and inner curves with tube 16 shells.

4. Trim the cake with roses, attaching each by piping a mound of icing on the back. Attach flowers in area where cakes join first, then add smaller flowers above and within garlands. Center the party table with this rosy masterpiece and wait for showers of compliments. Serves 20 guests, generously.

Plant a garden for a flower-lover

Is she (or he!) famous for having the most gorgeous flower garden in the neighborhood? Here's the perfect cake.

1. Do Color Flow trims in advance. Review page 116 for technique. Outline patterns for pickets and fence rails with tube 2, fill in with thinned icing and dry thoroughly. Use royal icing to "glue" the fence together in four sections, one for each side of cake. Dry again.

Draw a 3" x 4" rectangle as pattern for the five seed packets. "Paint" five popsicle sticks with thinned icing and dry. Peel paper off packets, turn over and attach a popsicle stick to the back of each with dots of un-thinned icing. Outline and fill in packets again, right over sticks. Dry.

2. Make royal icing flowers in advance, or go through your store of practice flowers and select appropriate blooms. Directions for flowers in the picture are in Chapter Six, page 92, directions for the zinnia are on page 79. Pipe the names on the seed packets with tube 1, then attach flowers with dots of royal icing. Trim with tube 65 leaves.

3. Bake and chill a cake in a long loaf pan, 16" x 4". Ice the sides in pale sky blue buttercream. Ice the top chocolate and roughen the surface with a spatula. Set on cake board. Frame top edge with tube 5 balls. Pipe mounds of icing on the backs of the fence sections and carefully press to sides of cake. Use tube 1 to pull out "grass" at base of fence. Stick seed packets into "ground" on top of cake. This amusing centerpiece serves 16 flower-lovers.

For a cute souvenir of the party, we put a stemmed icing rose in a little plastic watering pot and tied on a card for the guest of honor.

Use made-ahead flowers or pipe the favorites of the honored guest

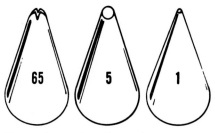

Two tubes edge the cake

Make a real splash on the Fourth of July!

Stars, stripes, red, white and blue tapers and a brilliant bouquet of icing flowers make this a cake to remember! This cake looks impressive, but plan ahead—you can do it in easy steps. Serve it on Memorial Day, the Fourth of July or any patriotic occasion. It will turn a holiday get-together into a gala celebration.

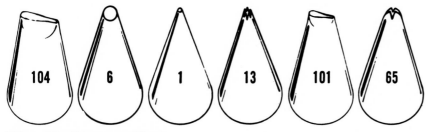

Pipe the flowers first

Do them in royal icing—they can be made weeks or even months ahead. Pipe the daisies with tube 104 petals and tube 6 centers. Use tubes 1 and 13 for the bachelor buttons. See pages 97 and 100. The scarlet zinnias are made with tube 101 petals just like the marigolds on page 100—just add a few tube 1 yellow dots in the centers when the flowers are finished. Pipe tube 65 leaves on florists' wire. When flowers are thoroughly dry, mount them on wire stems as shown on page 104. Use green floral tape to attach several leaves to each flower stem. Push into a block of styrofoam and set aside.

Make the Color Flow stars

Review the technique described on page 116 to make the stars. You will need twelve, but make a few extras in case of breakage.

Bake and decorate the cake

Before starting, get out your ring mold and decide on a small bowl or other container that will fit into the center opening to hold the flowers. We used an 11″ ring mold and a small white plastic bowl.

1. Bake and chill the cake, ice smoothly in buttercream and let icing set. Using the method on page 42, divide the side of the cake evenly into twelfths. You will need to do this three times—at base of cake, at top edge and at inner edge. Mark at these points with a toothpick, then connect the marks to form stripes.

2. Form six red stripes by filling in the marked areas with tube 16 stars, holding cone straight out from cake, and doing outer edges first. Use tube 19 to pipe a star border at base of cake.

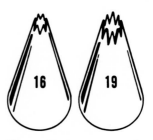

The cake is very quick to decorate

Put everything together

Pack flower container with Oasis (obtainable at your florist), or with styrofoam. Push in three tapers, then set container in center opening of cake. Starting with tallest flowers, arrange the red, white and blue bouquet by pushing in wire stems.

Pipe a mound of icing on back of each Color Flow star and gently press to white area of cake side. The stripes make it easy to cut the cake into twelve generous servings.

Here's a good example of how planning ahead can produce a spectacular centerpiece in easy stages.

A golden eagle
rests on a
star-studded cake.
Serve it with pride
on the Fourth!

Center a sheet cake with a golden eagle, surround him with sparkling stars and drape the cake sides with garlands in patriotic colors. You've created a smashing centerpiece for a Fourth of July celebration!

Make sugar trims in advance

Use star candy molds and a large eagle mold for the trims. Review the sugar molding directions on page 105. Tint most of the sugar mixture gold and small amounts red and blue, and mold the shapes. As soon as they're removed from molds, sprinkle with edible glitter for sparkle.

Since the eagle form is large, dry it about eight hours. When thoroughly dry, use tube 3 to pipe the red, white and blue stripes on the banner.

Bake and decorate the cake

Now that the trims are finished, the cake is very easy to decorate.

1. Bake two layers in 9″ x 13″ sheet cake pans. Chill, then fill and ice smoothly with buttercream. Divide top edge of cake into fourths on the long sides and thirds on the shorter sides and mark with a toothpick. Divide and mark base of cake into sixths on the long side and fourths on the shorter sides. Page 42 tells how. Transfer to cake board.

2. Pipe puffy tube 19 zigzag garlands from mark to mark at base of cake. Hold cone straight out and use light pressure at start of garland, increase pressure and lift tube as you near the center, then relax pressure at end. Frame bottom of garlands in blue icing with tube 3 and a tight "e" motion. Change to red icing and frame the tops of the garlands in the same way.

3. Use tube 13 to pipe the top border. First drop a tube 3 string guideline from mark to mark. Pipe reverse shells at top edge of cake. Following guidelines, pipe blue zigzags in curves, above them white zigzags and finally red zigzag curves. Pipe an upright shell between each garland and top with a rosette.

Center eagle on cake top, raising back slightly with mounds of icing. Pipe a dot of icing on the back of each star and arrange in a curve around eagle. This easy-to-serve sheet cake serves 24 patriots. Save the eagle as a memento of a golden summer day.

Make it a party!

Summertime is the best time to get together with friends for relaxed fun. So plan an all-American barbecue with hot dogs and hamburgers, baked beans and cole slaw. Or have a leisurely buffet lunch on the porch or terrace. Serve platters of sliced baked ham, roast beef and chicken. Add hot buttered rolls, fresh vegetable relishes and molded salads. For either celebration, bring out a big bowl of ripe strawberries for dessert—along with the stunning cake.

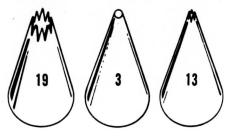

Star tubes do border designs accented with curves piped with a round tube

A cake for a gardener holds a harvest of vegetables!

As summer nears its close, have one last glorious outing on Labor Day—and make this spectacular harvest cake for the finale. It will be a reward for the hard-working gardeners who labored in the sun all season—and a delightful conversation piece for everyone.

While this cake looks very impressive, taken step by step with careful planning even a novice decorator can achieve it.

Make the cornucopia first

The cornucopia starts with a pointed ice cream cone and royal icing. Cut the cone about one-third of the way from the point, then put it back together again in a curve, using icing as glue. Cover with icing, filling in crack, and dry.

Cover cornucopia with curved shells

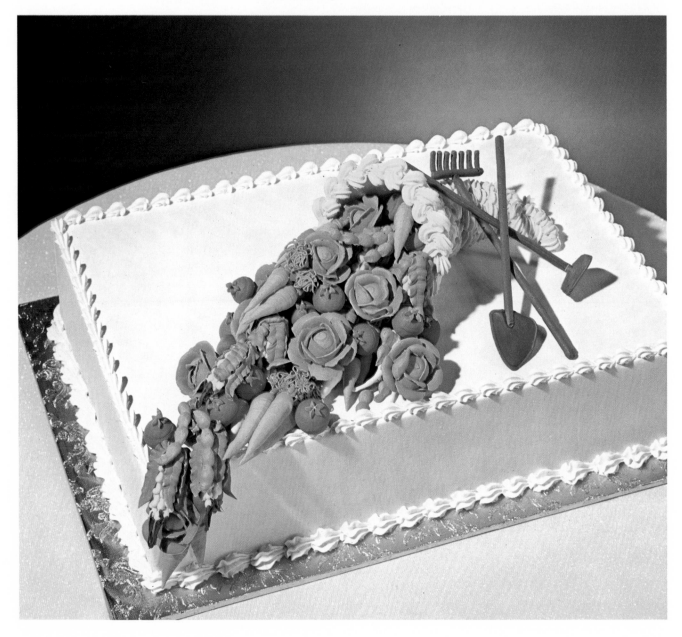

Now cover the cone with rows of tube 19 shells, starting at point. Finish the opening with more curved shells and dry.

Make the garden tools

These realistic little tools are made with Color Flow icing (see page 116). Patterns are in the Appendix, starting page 162. First pipe the handles on wax paper with tube 5 and icing straight from the batch. Tape rake teeth pattern to a curved form and pipe with tube 3. Outline spade and hoe with tube 1, then fill in with thinned icing. When all are thoroughly dry, attach handles with unthinned icing and dry again.

Pipe the vegetables

All the vegetables are piped on wax paper in buttercream, slightly stiffened with additional confectioners' sugar. Most are based on a simple ball shape. You'll find it fun to create this miniature harvest and will probably pipe some new varieties of your own.

For the peas, first pipe a slender strip about 2" long on wax paper with tube 104. On this pod, pipe round balls for peas with tube 3.

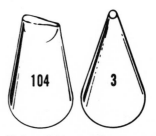

Tubes 104 and 3 pipe peas

The cabbages start with a tube 5 ball on a flower nail. Then add tube 104 "petals" for leaves, just as you would for a rose, as shown on page 101. Leave top of ball exposed.

Pull out a long cone shape with tube 5 for carrots and parsnips, and groove lightly with a knife. Tomatoes are just tube 5 red balls.

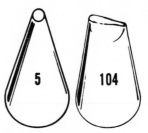

Tomatoes, parsnips, carrots and cabbage start with tube 5

The corn starts with a long yellow shell piped with tube 21. Fill in the grooves with tube 3 dots, then pull out green tube 65 leaves for husks.

Freeze all the vegetables until you are ready to assemble the cake.

Prepare the sheet cake

Bake two layers in 9" x 13" pans and chill. Fill, then ice smoothly in buttercream. Set on a foil-covered cake board and pipe base shell border with tube 21, top shell border with tube 19.

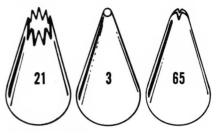

Use three tubes to pipe corn

Put everything together

Assembling all the parts of this tableau is the most fun. Set cornucopia on cake top, securing with two or three mounds of icing. Now pipe a long heavy curve of icing with tube 21, starting within cornucopia and extending to corner of cake. Arrange the frozen vegetables, using mounds of icing to hold them up as needed.

When you have completed the composition, add the finishing touches. Do carrot tops with loops and curves piped with tube 1. Use the same tube to pipe corn silk. Pipe a little green star with tube 13 on each tomato. Casually lean the tools on the cornucopia. The frozen vegetables will thaw in just a few minutes. Enjoy the harvest! This gardener's dream cake will serve 24.

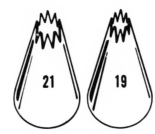

Star tubes pipe the borders

Add the finishing touches

Wreath a holiday cake with brilliant marzipan fruits

Marzipan, that rich almond-flavored confection, is truly the traditional sweet for Christmas. For many centuries gifts of marzipan have been exchanged during the holidays. Now see how marzipan fruits can glorify a simple cake!

Most decorators are amazed at how easily marzipan can be formed into various shapes. If you've ever worked with modeling clay as a child, you can model marzipan. So assemble the simple ingredients you need and mix a batch, then create this colorful Della Robbia wreath. This craft is so simple and enjoyable the children can help.

MARZIPAN RECIPE

1 cup almond paste (8-ounce can)   3 cups confectioners' sugar
2 egg whites, unbeaten   ½ teaspoon rum flavor

Knead almond paste by hand in bowl. Add egg whites, mix well. Continue kneading as you add sugar, 1 cup at a time, and flavoring until marzipan feels like heavy pie dough. Stored properly, marzipan dough will keep for months. Cover with plastic wrap, then place in tightly-sealed container in refrigerator. After storing, let stand at room temperature until soft enough to work. If too stiff, soften with a drop or two of warmed corn syrup.

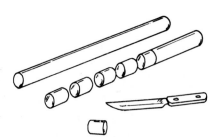

Roll into cylinder and cut into even pieces for uniform sizes

How to tint marzipan

For the fruits in this wreath we are using five colors,—red, yellow, orange, pale green and grape color—so divide the marzipan into five portions. As you work with one portion, keep others covered. Knead liquid food color into original mixture, a drop at a time, until you arrive at the tint you want.

How to form the fruits

Dust your work surface well with confectioners' sugar, and form a tinted portion of marzipan into a cylinder about ¾" in diameter by rolling it with your palms. Cut the cylinder into ¾" pieces. This will keep the fruits a uniform size. Now roll each piece between your palms into a ball shape. Elongate the ball into an oval for lemons, pinch and roll one end for pears, roll bananas into long ovals, then pinch ends. Roll lemons and oranges over a grater for rough texture and cut a groove into peaches with the dull side of a knife. Use cloves for stems. To give a blush to peaches and pears, touch a damp cloth to red food color and rub on fruit. Mark bananas with brown food color.

Grapes are modeled with a different method. Pinch off a little marzipan, form it into a leaf shape with your hands and curve over your finger. Break off tiny pieces of marzipan, roll into balls and attach to leaf shape by dipping into egg white, then pressing to leaf, starting at pointed tip. Let fruits dry on wax paper.

How to glaze the fruit

For a high shine, mix ½ cup of corn syrup with two tablespoons of water and bring to a boil. Brush over the fruit and allow to dry on wax paper.

Decorate the cake

The cake is decorated very simply to set off the beautiful fruit. Bake, fill and ice a two-layer 10" round cake. Set on serving tray, then pipe a rippled base border, using tube 104 and a back-and-forth movement.

Arrange fruit on cake, securing with mounds of icing where needed. Fill out the design with a few tube 67 leaves. Set a tall taper in the center. Your Christmas masterpiece is complete and will serve 14.

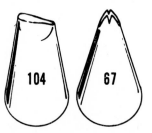

A simple border and a few leaves finish the cake

**A continental-style cake trimmed with
a bounty of fruit and vegetable miniatures**

After you've had the fun of modeling fruits from marzipan like those shown on the cake on page 84, you'll enjoy the challenge of creating these miniature masterpieces. These little fruits and vegetables have a startling realism, easily achieved with this workable material. Heap them on a glazed cake and you'll create a real showpiece!

Model the marzipan fruits and vegetables first

Make the recipe for marzipan on page 85 and review the general directions—then start your project.

Some of the fruits are painted. Dilute food color with a little vodka or a white liqueur and brush the color on with an artist's brush. The alcohol in the liqueur makes for quick drying.

Whole apples, oranges and peaches, grapes and bananas are formed just as described on page 85. The *limes* are modeled from green marzipan, just like a lemon.

The cantaloupe starts with a ball of orange marzipan. Cut it in half and indent the center with the round end of an orange stick. Break off a small piece of untinted marzipan and work it between your fingers into a flat thin disk. Wrap it around the half ball and groove the outside with the dull side of a small knife. Paint a light beige, dry, then pipe the seeds with royal icing and tube 1.

The watermelon is formed by molding a rounded pink cylinder about 2½" x ¾". Cover it with untinted marzipan just as you did for the cantaloupe, then with green marzipan. Paint darker green stripes on the outside. Let the melon set up for an hour or so, then cut in slices with a cheese cutter. Add tube 1 royal icing seeds.

Half-apples and peaches start by forming whole fruits. Use light orange marzipan for the peach, untinted for the apple. Refine the shapes with an orange stick. Let the fruits set, then cut in half. Hollow the center of the peach and insert a little ball of brown marzipan. Paint the outside of the apple with red food color, dry, then pipe royal icing seeds.

For the pineapple, cut off a 1¼" slice from your basic cylinder of yellow marzipan. Form into an upright rounded shape and make criss-cross grooves with a knife. Work green marzipan into leaf shapes, then attach to top by dipping in egg white.

Model the pumpkin from a 2" piece cut off the basic cylinder and groove.

Carrots are just long pointed cylinders, grooved. Roll little balls for *peas.* Work a small piece of green marzipan into a thin strip, brush with egg white and wrap the peas in it.

The green pepper looks so real! Form a ball of marzipan and cut it in half. Hollow out with an orange stick and shape with your fingers. Add royal icing seeds.

Glaze all fruits and vegetables as directed on page 85.

Bake and decorate the cake

Bake a cake in a turk's head mold, 8" in diameter, and a single layer in a 10" round pan. A pound cake recipe is a good choice. Prepare a glaze by heating one cup of apricot jam to boiling and strain. While glaze is still hot, brush on the 10" layer, set turk's head cake on top and brush it with glaze. Let glaze set, then pipe a bulb border with tube 5 and simple side trim with tube 2. Arrange your beautiful fruits and vegetables, using a little icing to secure where necessary. Bravo!

Your continental masterpiece serves 18.

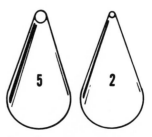

Simple piping creates European-style trim

Bake a Christmas treat just for the children

Won't they love this bright holiday cake! A gaily dressed gingerbread boy and girl stand on top and a host of cookie children circle the cake. Decorate it as the centerpiece for a merry Christmas party.

Do the gingerbread children first

1. Use your favorite recipe or the one below—it's especially fragrant and spicy and makes a firm cookie.

GRANDMA'S GINGERBREAD

5 to 5½ cups all purpose flour	1 teaspoon cloves
1 teaspoon baking soda	1 cup shortening
1 teaspoon salt	1 cup sugar
2 teaspoons ginger	1¼ cups unsulphured molasses
2 teaspoons cinnamon	2 eggs, beaten
1 teaspoon nutmeg	

Thoroughly mix flour, soda, salt and spices. Melt shortening in large saucepan. Add sugar, molasses, and eggs, mix well. Cool slightly, then add four cups of the dry ingredients and mix well. Turn mixture onto lightly floured surface. Knead in remaining dry ingredients by hand. Roll dough to ⅛" thickness.

Use 5½" and 2½" cutters to shape the dough. You will need about two dozen small cookies. Lay moistened popsicle sticks on a greased cookie sheet, and place larger cookies on top of them so sticks extend to insert in cake top. Transfer small cookies to a greased baking sheet. Bake all cookies at 375°F for about eight to ten minutes. Allow the cookies to cool on baking sheets a few moments before removing them to cool completely on wire racks.

2. Decorate the cookies in the Color Flow technique as explained on page 116. Outline all colored areas, allow outlines to dry, then fill in with thinned icing. Use icing right from the batch to add details. On large cookies use tube 2 to pipe features, buttons, "rick rack" trim on apron and girl's curly hair. Use tube 1 to pipe details on tiny cookies.

Bake and decorate the cake

1. Bake a two-layer cake in 10" round pans, each layer about 2" high. Chill, fill and ice smoothly in buttercream and set on cake board.

2. Border with tube 21 stars in alternating colors. Lift the tube as the stars build up for a puffy effect. Pipe tailored, interlaced stringwork below the top border with tube 3.

3. Now secure tiny cookie children to cake side, piping a mound of icing on the back of each. Push popsicle sticks on big cookies into cake top and call the children! This holiday treat serves 14.

With the extra cookie dough left from the cake trims, bake extra boy and girl cookies and decorate them like the cookies on the cake. These make delightful take-home favors, and can serve as place cards, too, if you pipe a child's name on each.

Tiny tubes trim the cookies

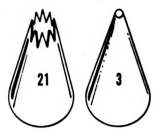

Color adds charm to simple borders

Fun-to-do

cookies

make the sweetest

tree trims

For centuries the Christmas tree has been the very center of the holiday celebration—and a tree hung with decorated cookies has a special homey charm. More than half the fun is in creating the cookie trims. This is definitely a group project. The whole family and close friends, too, can gather in the kitchen to mix the dough, sniff the wonderful aroma from the oven, and then sit down to add the bright icing trims. The very youngest child can help stir, lick the bowl and fill in icing. Even the clean-up is fun when you do it together! You'll probably need at least two evenings to create the cookie trims—one for baking, one for decorating. They'll be very happy hours.

Bake a big batch of cookies

Use the recipe on page 18—it will make about four dozen large cookies, 4½" to 6"—or any favorite recipe that makes a firm cookie. If you need more cookies (and you'll be surprised at how many disappear as they come out of the oven) mix a second or third batch. Do not double the recipe, it is too difficult to mix a larger batch.

We used large cutters, but get out your collection, and cut out as many different shapes as possible. After you've transfered the cut-out cookies to baking sheets, cut a hole near the top of each with a plastic soda straw or any large round tube. For really big cookies like the angels, we cut two holes. Bake and cool the cookies.

Decorating is the most fun

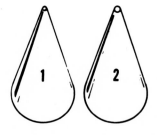

For the cookies on our tree, we used Color Flow icing and the technique described on page 116. First the colored areas were outlined with tube 2, then filled in with thinned icing and a cone with cut tip. Let the cookies dry for about an hour at this point before adding details with tubes 1 or 2. Notice that in some of the designs the cookie is not completely covered, letting the baked surface become part of the trim.

Relax, enjoy, and let your imagination take over. A round cookie can become a wreath or a smiling face, a star, a snowflake or a flower. Turn a gingerbread man into Santa Claus, a gingerbread lady into his wife. Trim an oval-shaped cookie so it becomes your favorite cartoon character, an angel, one of the three kings. There'll be a few mistakes, quickly eaten, and lots of happy surprises.

When all the cookies are decorated, thread white cloth-covered florists' wire through the holes and form a hook for hanging from the ends. We tied narrow red ribbon into little bows and attached them to the cookies with icing to cover the holes and wire.

When you trim the tree with these treasures you'll all declare it never looked as beautiful—and you'll make a tradition of creating unique cookie trims for the tree.

CHAPTER SIX

Piped flowers...as beautiful as those growing in a garden

The most beautiful trim a cake can have is flowers. We can't say a piped flower is as lovely as a fresh blossom, but in realistic form and color the icing flower does approach the beauty of its namesake.

This chapter shows just how to pipe the most popular flowers. By following correct techniques you'll find it easy and exciting to create a whole garden. After you've mastered these flowers, study fresh flowers, and the pictures in seed catalogs. You'll be able to reproduce many more blossoms by varying the techniques.

For most flowers, we recommend royal icing. It will hold the crisp forms of the petals, the flowers may be piped even months ahead and be ready to put on a cake when you are, and they are very easy to arrange in bouquets, sprays and clusters.

Be sure to save the best of your practice flowers. Store them in a covered box and bring them out to add their beauty to cakes you need to decorate in a hurry.

Decorate a cake with a spray of roses

Here is an exquisite cake, quite simple to do, that features a spray of life-like roses. Decorate it for a birthday, anniversary, or any occasion you wish to make special.

1. Bake a 10" two-layer round cake, each layer about 2" high. Chill, fill and ice with white buttercream. After the icing has set, make a recipe of Quick Poured Fondant (page 23), tint pink and pour over the cake, starting in top center and circling the cake so it flows over the side. Have a spatula at hand to touch up bare spots. Let fondant set, then divide and mark side of cake into twelfths, about 1" up from base. See page 42 for method. Gently press a 4" cookie cutter on top center of cake, or trace a 4" paper circle. Transfer cake to serving tray.

2. Practice making royal icing rosebuds, page 96, and roses, page 101. You'll need about 20 buds and six roses. Pipe the buds with tube 104 and a brush-striped cone. Add tube 2 sepals. Pipe roses with tube 104. Set flowers aside to dry thoroughly.

3. Use buttercream for trim. Outline the marked circle on top of cake with tube 6. When this has set, add color to deepen the remaining fondant, and pour to fill circle. Drop a tube 2 string guideline on side of cake from mark to mark to position ruffle. Pipe a tube 16 base shell border. Pipe the ruffle with tube 104, holding wide end of tube against cake, other end flaring out. Swivel hand up and down as you follow guideline. Directly above ruffle, pipe a tight zigzag garland with tube 16. Drop triple tube 2 strings, then add dots above string. Complete the border with tube 16 fleurs-de-lis, finishing each with a rosette.

4. Pipe a curved spray of stems on cake top with tube 2. Write name in circle with tube 2, and pipe tube 16 shells around circle. Arrange the roses and buds, piping a mound of icing on back of each to attach. Finish with tube 67 leaves. This delicate masterpiece serves 14.

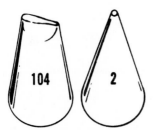

*Royal icing pipes lasting,
easy-to-arrange flowers*

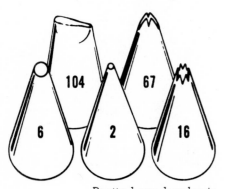

*Pretty base border is
edged with ruffles*

**Drop flowers are
fast and fun to pipe**

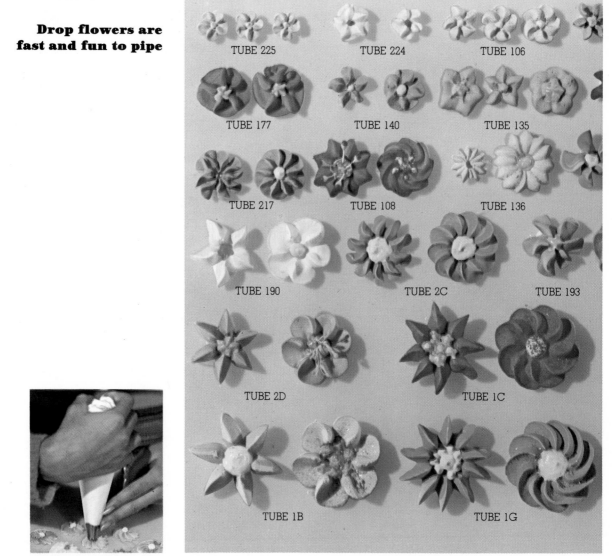

TUBE 225   TUBE 224   TUBE 106

TUBE 177   TUBE 140   TUBE 135

TUBE 217   TUBE 108   TUBE 136

TUBE 190   TUBE 2C   TUBE 193

TUBE 2D   TUBE 1C

TUBE 1B   TUBE 1G

*For a flower with furled petals,
start with your hand turned
to the left as shown above*

225   190

*These tubes pipe a tray
full of flowers in minutes*

Start your flower-piping project with drop flowers. These are called production flowers, because simply one squeeze of the hand and you've made a pretty little blossom. The pictures and accompanying tube numbers above show just some of the forms these flowers can take.

Let's do our practice with tubes 190 and 225. Tint royal icing in several pretty colors and keep well-covered until ready to use. Pipe a few stripes of icing on back of a cookie sheet, press wax paper over.

Hold tube 190 straight up, as shown on page 32. Lightly touch tube to surface, squeeze, stop squeezing, then pull away. For a variation as shown in the second flower, turn your hand to the left as far as possible and squeeze as you turn it to the right. Stop squeezing, then pull away. If the petals are too thick, you have applied too much pressure.

Make a smaller flower with tube 225, as shown at the top of the picture. Turn hand to left, hold cone straight up, squeeze while turning hand to right, stop pressure and lift up.

When you've completed a tray of flowers, add stamens in the centers with a plain round tube. We used tube 1 for the tiny tube 225 flowers, tube 3 for the tube 190 flowers. When flowers are dry, slide a spatula under the wax paper and peel paper off flowers.

An abundance of bright drop flowers make this little cake just as pretty as a wedding cake. Give it added importance by baking it in Mini-Tier pans and using the little Mini-Tier Separator set.

1. Pipe royal icing drop flowers on the back of a cookie sheet with tubes 190 and 225. Use the "hand turned to left" technique as shown on opposite page. Add tube 2 stamens in centers of flowers. Dry flowers.

2. Bake single-layer tiers in 5″, 6½″ and 8″ pans. Three pans hold one cake mix. Chill, then ice each tier. Set 8″ tier on cake board or serving tray, place two smaller tiers on 5½″ and 7″ separator plates. Insert clear legs into projections below separator plates. Carefully center 6½″ tier over 8″ tier, and gently press until legs touch cake board. Position top tier in the same manner.

3. Each tier is decorated in buttercream with the same borders. Circle the base of the tier with tube 17 zigzag garlands. Go back and pipe a star with the same tube between each garland. Tube 67 pipes the ruffly top borders. Pipe it just as if you were making a shell border, but keep your pressure even.

4. Now deck the cake with flowers. Attach trios of flowers to sides of two lower tiers with dots of icing. Pipe a heavy curve of icing from each leg of separator plates to edge of cake and press in flowers. Push a birthday candle into top tier and pipe a mound of icing around it. Press in flowers. Now trim the flowers with tube 65 leaves, using thinned icing and drawing out to points.

This impressive little treat will serve twelve—cut two servings from the top tier, four from the middle tier, and six from the base.

Trim a dainty tier cake for a birthday

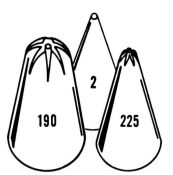

Pipe flowers with tubes 190 and 225, add tube 2 centers

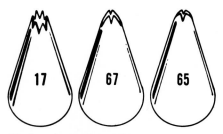

Do borders with tubes 17 and 67, finish with tube 65 leaves

Continue practice on the back of a cookie sheet

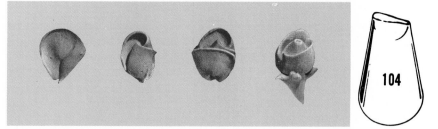

The rosebud, one of the sweetest flowers to grace a cake. To make it in royal icing, hold tube 104 at a 45° angle to the surface, wide end touching, and squeeze lightly as you turn your hand to the right to form a little cup. Keep tube in same position and squeeze lightly again. The rolled, interlocking bud will form itself inside the cup. Add a final, outer petal. Hold wide end of tube on left side of bud at base. Squeeze lightly as you lift tube and come down on other side of flower. Finish by piping a sepal, tiny green points meeting in a cone with tube 3. See how this little blossom enhances the cake on page 93.

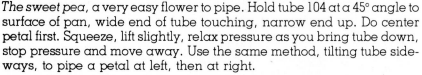

The sweet pea, a very easy flower to pipe. Hold tube 104 at a 45° angle to surface of pan, wide end of tube touching, narrow end up. Do center petal first. Squeeze, lift slightly, relax pressure as you bring tube down, stop pressure and move away. Use the same method, tilting tube sideways, to pipe a petal at left, then at right.

A sweet pea cluster is often used to drape gracefully from top to side of a cake. See the stunning wedding cake on page 161. First, give a base to the cluster. With tube 6, or any large tube, pipe a zigzag diamond, top point on top of cake, lower point on side of cake. Pipe a second, smaller diamond on top of first. Press dried sweet peas around edge of base, then fill in entire base with flowers to form a rounded cluster. Pipe a few tube 65 leaves to finish.

Blossoms to pipe on a flower nail

Many flowers are piped on a number 7 flower nail, a convenient little turntable. First attach a 2″ wax paper square to the nail. Cut a few dozen of these, and place in a pile. Pipe a dot of icing on the nail and touch it to the pile of squares to attach. After the flower is piped, slide it off the nail to a tray to dry, and attach another square.

Hold the nail between thumb and forefinger of your left hand and slowly turn it counter clockwise as you press out petals with right hand. Flowers can be piped very quickly in an assembly-line technique.

Flowers to make on a flower nail

The wild rose is quick to pipe and a very pretty cake trim. Start with a wax paper square attached to your flower nail and tube 104. Hold tube with wide end touching surface at center of nail, narrow end lifted very slightly. Squeeze lightly as you bring the tube out toward edge of nail, then back to center. Lift your hand just a little to give the petal a cupped appearance. Turn nail slightly with your left hand and pipe a second petal. Continue for five petals. Finish the flower by pulling out tube 1 stamens in the center, cone held straight up. See how sweet these flowers look on the cake on page 12.

The spring violet is piped with tube 101. Hold tube with wide end of tube in center of nail, narrow end lifted slightly. Bring tube out and back to center to pipe a narrow petal about ½" long, turning nail slowly. Now pipe two more petals the same way, but only ¼" long. Complete by piping two more ½" petals and adding two tube 1 dots in the center.

The daisy gives a fresh flowery look to any cake. First pipe a little dot of icing in the center of your nail to mark point where petals meet. Hold tube 102 straight up near edge of nail, narrow end of tube pointing toward edge. Press lightly as you move tube to center. Stop pressure, lift tube and turn nail slightly to pipe a second petal, just as you did the first. Continue piping petals until you've done eleven or twelve in a complete circle, then pipe a tube 3 dot in center. For a sparkly look, moisten your finger, dip in yellow-tinted sugar and press on dot.

Pipe a cosmos, a showy summer flower in a similar fashion to the daisy. Use tube 104 to pipe just eight petals, pulling them from edge to center of nail just as you did for the daisy. As soon as petals are piped, use the tip of a damp artist's brush to groove the petals. Center the flower with a tube 10 dot, then flatten the dot with a fingertip. Pipe a circle of tube 1 dots around the center.

Trim a sunny cake
with springtime daisies

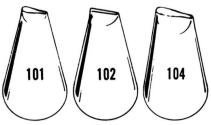

Pipe three sizes of daisies

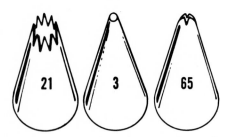

*Finish the cake with
quick borders and leaves*

1. Pipe the daisies in royal icing in advance, just as described on page 97. Use tubes 101, 102 and 104 for the petals for three sizes of flowers. Pipe center dot on the tube 101 flowers with tube 1, use tube 3 for dots on others. Dry flowers on curved forms as shown on page 104.

2. Bake a two-layer, 8" square cake. Chill layers, then fill and ice with buttercream. Set on ruffle-edged cake board. Make marks with a tooth-pick on top edge of all four sides of cake about 2" in from the corners.

3. Pipe a base border of puffy shells with tube 21. Drop curved string guidelines from marks on top edge of cake with green icing and tube 3. Pipe reverse shell top border with tube 21. (See page 38.)

Now trim the cake with flowers. Attach each by piping a little mound of icing on the back, then pressing gently to cake. Graduate sizes at base, keeping largest flowers at corners. Use largest flowers for center of garlands on cake sides, moving up to smallest daisies. Set a little cherub figure on top of cake to announce spring, then trim with smallest blossoms. Trim the flowers with tube 65 leaves. Tuck tube under the petals and pull out points. This quick-to-do treat serves twelve.

Now that you've had practice in piping flowers, design some original cake creations and trim them with your made-ahead blossoms. Just simple borders and pretty tints of icing make beautiful cakes when the blossoms are added. The royal icing flowers will soften somewhat as they rest on the buttercream-covered cake. Bring cakes to friends as just-for-fun gifts. They'll be amazed at your artistry!

Butterflies flutter above a blooming cake

This brilliant cake really says it with flowers! A cascade of marigolds and bachelor buttons curves from top to base in colors that rival fresh blossoms from your garden.

1. Make the butterflies in the Color Flow technique, using patterns in Appendix, starting page 162. First read page 116 for general directions, then outline wings with tube 1 and fill in with cut cone. Add tube 1 dots at wing edges and dry. Lay a fine wire on wax paper-covered surface and pipe a tear-drop shape for body over the end with black royal icing. Immediately insert wings into body and prop with cotton balls to dry at an angle. Insert two cut-off artificial stamens for antenna, or use short pieces of wire and tip each with a dot of black icing.

2. Tint royal icing in brilliant yellow, gold and orange and pipe marigolds just as shown on page 100. Use blue royal icing and directions on the same page to do the bachelor buttons. When flowers are dry, pipe a spike with tube 4 on the backs of about one-fourth of the marigolds. Page 104 shows how.

3. Bake, fill and ice a two-layer, 10" round cake. Do garland borders at base with tight zigzags of tube 16. Pipe top shell border with same tube. Pipe tube 16 curves of icing to form a scallop pattern on cake top.

4. Now trim the cake with flowers in a swirling cascade. Mark a curve on cake top, extending down side, with a toothpick. Pipe a thick curve of icing on top of cake and fill in with marigolds, piping a dot of icing on back of each to secure. Use spiked marigolds for curve on side. Add accents of bachelor buttons, then trim with tube 65 leaves. Twist wires on butterflies together, wrap with clear plastic and insert in cake. The butterflies will quiver with every breeze! Serves 14.

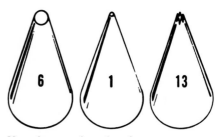

Just one tube pipes borders.
Two tubes pipe
the brilliant marigolds

Use these tubes for the
blue bachelor buttons

More flowers to pipe on a number 7 nail

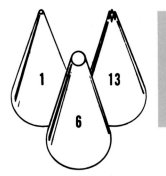

The bachelor button is piped with two tints of blue royal icing. Using pale blue, first pipe a round mound of icing with tube 6, then pull out pointed dots in the center with tube 1. Change to deeper blue icing and tube 13. Pipe short star petals all around dots, continuing until the mound is completely covered. Add a few more petals for a full look.

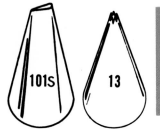

The golden marigold. Pipe petals with tube 101s. Touch wide end of tube to center of nail, narrow end lifted slightly. Keep a continuous back and forth movement to pipe a circle of slender petals, each about ½″ long. Turn nail slowly as you pipe. Pipe two more rows of petals, one on top of the other, the petals in each row shorter than the last. Complete the flower by filling the center with tube 13 stars, holding cone straight up.

The pansy is piped with yellow and violet royal icing. Fit two cones with tube 104. Brush-stripe one with violet paste color, applying straight up from narrow end of tube. Spatula-stripe cone midway between narrow and wide end of tube with violet icing, then fill with yellow icing. Brush-stripe second cone with violet paste color, applying one stripe straight up from narrow end of tube, a second stripe straight up from wide end of tube. Now hold cone with yellow icing straight up, wide end of tube in center of nail, and pipe two round petals. Pipe two more petals almost covering first two. Use cone with violet icing, and jiggle hand slightly to pipe a large ruffled petal below. Add a yellow tear drop shape in center with tube 1.

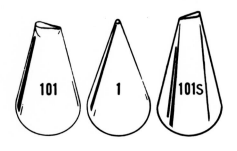

The dainty apple blossom petals are piped with tube 101 exactly the same as for the wild rose on page 97. Add a group of dots in center with tube 1. Make the blue *forget-me-not* the same way but use tube 101s. Add a single tube 1 dot in center.

Here's how to pipe a perfect, full-blown rose

The rose is really the queen of flowers—it adds regal beauty to any cake. Here's the easy, professional way to reproduce it in icing. Fit a decorating cone with tube 12 and another with tube 104, then fill cones with pink royal icing.

1. Hold tube 12 straight up and pipe a high dome of icing. Use heavy pressure, then gradually relax pressure as you move upward. Keep tube buried in icing before stopping pressure and moving away.

2. Hold tube 104 in the position shown above, narrow end up, just at the top of the dome. Turn the nail as you pipe a ribbon of icing, moving the tube up, around and down to make a pointed, cone-shaped center.

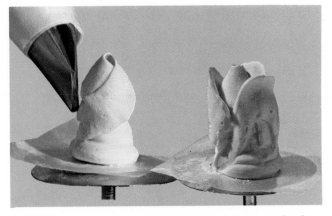

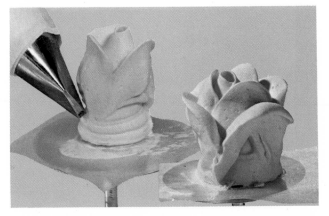

3. Hold cone against dome so it points straight from your shoulder, narrow end up and turned out slightly. Pipe three standing petals, moving hand up and down in an arch as you turn the nail.

4. Hold wide end of tube against dome a little below the three petals, pointing narrow end of tube outward. Pipe four petals, again moving hand up and down in an arch as you turn the nail.

Furl petals

5. Finish with seven overlapping petals at the base of the dome, narrow end of tube pointing nearly straight out. Slide paper off nail to dry.

For a rose with daintily furled petals, dip your fingers in cornstarch, and gently pinch the petals in the last two rows to a point. Do this as soon as the rose is piped.

A stunning cake for a summertime party

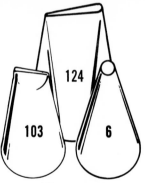

*Three tubes pipe
flowers and leaves*

Use only one tube for trim

Nasturtiums, as brilliant as a summer sunrise, curve across this simple cake. The flowers may be made even weeks ahead, then the decorating can be done in a hurry.

1. Tint royal icing in brilliant hues, and pipe the flowers in advance, just as shown on the next page. Use a 1⅝" lily nail and tube 103 for the petals. Pipe a tube 6 dot in the center of the flower to anchor the petals. Mount several of the flowers on wire stems, pipe spikes on the backs of about six flowers. (See page 104.)

Make the distinctive nasturtium leaf with tube 124 on a number 7 flower nail. Touch wide end of tube to center of nail, cone held straight up and narrow end of tube almost touching nail. Turn nail as you use light pressure to form the flat leaf, then stop pressure and move away. Vein the leaves with the tip of a damp artist's brush. After drying, mount about six of the leaves on wire stems, just as you would a flower.

2. Bake two layers in 9" oval pans. Chill, then fill and ice smoothly. Mark freehand "C" shapes on top and side of cake with a toothpick. Place cake on a serving tray.

3. Do all decorating with tube 16. Pipe shell borders at base and top of cake. Pipe the "C" curves, then go back and over-pipe them with back-and-forth movements. Arrange the flowers on the cake top, securing with small mounds of icing. Twist stems of wired flowers and leaves together, wrap in clear plastic and push into cake toward the rear of the arrangement. Use spiked flowers to trim side of cake, then attach leaves to cake with icing. Serve this glowing masterpiece to twelve.

Pipe these flowers in a lily nail

Trumpet-shaped flowers like those on this page must be piped in a lily nail to achieve the proper form. Use two-piece plastic nails that come in four sizes for flowers from little to large. Put a square of foil on the top of the lower portion of nail and press upper portion of nail into it. Then pipe the flower in the foil-lined nail, turning the stem just as a number 7 nail. When finished, lift out foil and let the flower dry as you pipe others. Peel foil off dried flowers.

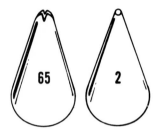

The bluebell. Line a 1¼″ lily nail with foil. Insert tube 65 within nail and pull a slender leaf into a point. Pipe two more leaves, evenly spaced, overlapping at base. Now pipe a leaf between each, for six petals. Pipe a dot of icing in center of flower with tube 2, and push in a few artificial stamens. Lift foil out of nail and set aside to dry.

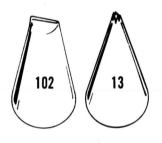

The ruffled petunia is piped with tube 102. Line a 1⅝″ lily nail with foil. Insert tube into nail, wide end down. Squeeze lightly as you move up, turning nail slowly and jiggling hand to form ruffles. Move back down to base of nail again. Repeat for five petals, even in size. Pipe a green star with tube 13 in center of flower and push in a few artificial stamens. Lift foil out to dry.

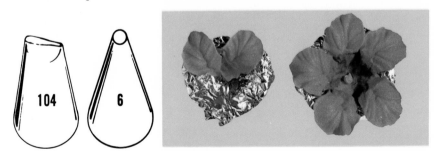

**How to pipe
the brilliant nasturtium**

Pipe this favorite garden flower almost the same as the petunia, above. Line a 1⅝″ lily nail with foil and fit your decorating cone with tube 104. Pipe the petals as narrow as possible at the base and let the tips curl over the nail edge slightly. Pipe a tube 6 dot in center of flower to join petals firmly, lift out foil and dry. With a small artist's brush, paint streaks of contrasting food color at base of petals. Pipe another tube 6 dot in center, insert a few artificial stamens, dry again and peel off foil. *Caution:* this is a fragile flower so handle with care.

How to display royal icing flowers at their graceful best

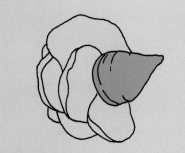

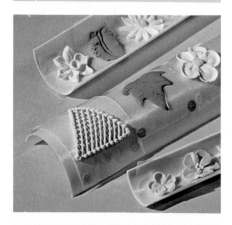

Mount blooms on florists' wire stems

To make a spray, a bouquet or a little nosegay, put stems on your flowers. After they've been piped in royal icing and dried, cut a number of lengths of green cloth-covered florists' wire. Lightweight or small flowers can use fine wire, heavier flowers, like the rose, require stiffer wire. Pipe a tube 6 mound of green royal icing on a small wax paper square, stick the end of a wire into it, and smooth the icing onto the wire with a damp artist's brush to form a calyx. Turn upright and stick the other end of the wire into a block of styrofoam to dry, then peel off the wax paper square, pipe a mound of royal icing on the calyx and gently press the flower onto it. Dry again. Now the flower can be arranged in any fashion you like. See bouquets on pages 78 and 140. Use an assembly line technique to attach stems to many flowers in just a short time.

To give stems to leaves, pipe a small mound of icing on wax paper. Lay the wire on it and pipe leaf directly over the wire so it becomes the center vein of leaf. You may add a leaf at side by letting icing build up on the wire before you pull leaf to a point. When dry, peel off paper.

How to attach flowers to side of cake

Do it the easy way by piping a "spike" of royal icing to the back of any large or heavy flower piped in royal icing and dried. Use tube 5 or 6. When spike is thoroughly dry, push it into the iced cake and it will hold securely as part of a cascade or spray. (Lightweight or small flowers may simply be attached to the side of a cake with a little mound of icing.)

Curve petals for a pretty natural look

Flower formers are washable plastic curves in graduated sizes. As soon as the flower is piped, slide it off the nail and dry it, still on its square of paper, within or over the formers. Result: blossoms with curved petals. You may make your own former if you like, by slicing the cardboard core of a roll of paper towels in half but the formers give you more versatility. Use them for other motifs you wish to curve, also.

Frame your flowers with natural-looking leaves

Study nature for the leaves appropriate to the flower. For clusters of small leaves, pipe stems on cake surface, then add tube 65 leaves, holding tube at a 45° angle to the surface. For large leaves, use tube 67 or 70, and pipe just the same as small leaves. By hesitating as the icing builds up, the tube will create a ruffled leaf. Holly leaves are piped with tube 67 or 70. As soon as a few are piped, use a damp artist's brush to pull out points. Remember—use thinned buttercream for all leaves piped on the cake.

CHAPTER SEVEN

Sugar molds...
fun and
easy to do

Here's an aspect of decorating that's pure enjoyment! Just dampen sugar, tinted as you wish, pack into a plastic mold and turn out cute shapes that can serve as party favors, cake trims, candy containers, tree trims or whatever your imagination can dream up. It's an especially good craft for children—even their first efforts are successful. Best of all, the little sugar forms last almost indefinitely.

1. Mix one egg white, lightly stirred, with two and a half pounds of granulated sugar. Knead with your hands a minute or two until sugar is evenly damp. Add liquid food color, as desired, and knead again.

You may store unused portions of the mixture, tightly wrapped in a plastic bag, in the refrigerator. Knead again before using, and if necessary, add a drop or two of water.

2. Pack the mixture firmly into a mold. Make sure all indentations are filled. Use a spatula to level the surface.

3. Place a piece of stiff cardboard over the mold (a small cake circle is handy for this), turn over, tap mold with a spatula and lift off. Air-dry about five hours, or dry in a 200°F oven about an hour. If you are using the same mold more than four times, dust it with cornstarch before using again to prevent sugar from sticking to the mold.

4. For a two-color mold, carefully pack sugar of one tint into mold, brush off any loose crumbs with an artist's brush, then complete filling mold with second tint.

How to mold a perky duckling

Mold the two halves of the duckling and dry. Cement the halves together with royal icing tinted to match the sugar, and dry again. Now dress up the little bird. Paint her beak with thinned royal icing, pipe the round blue eyes with tube 5 and tie a ribbon around her neck with tube 101. Attach a few made-ahead drop flowers to make a pretty Easter bonnet. Present this little pet to a child and watch his eyes light up!

Mix sugar and egg white

Pack into mold

Unmold immediately

Special effects with two tints

105

Sugar molds make spectacular Christmas trims!

Aren't these ornaments beautiful? Set aside an evening or two before the holidays and let the children help you turn out a dozen or more. Christmas will be even merrier! Use the tinted sugar mixture on page 105. Most of the trims are molded in two-piece egg molds in 5″, 4½″ and 3″ sizes, and in ball molds 3″ and 4½″ in diameter. We also molded a 2″ bell.

**How to mold
a hollow sugar form**

Pack the two halves of the egg or ball mold with sugar mixture and level with a spatula. Unmold on a small piece of stiff cardboard. Immediately cut off a section of a molded half-form by drawing a taut thread through it. This will be the opening. Leave the cut-off portion in position. Allow the molds to dry about an hour and a half.

Now place the half-form in your palm by up-ending the cardboard. Hold it *gently*, do not press! With a teaspoon, scoop out damp sugar from the flat surface, starting in center. Leave a shell about ¼″ thick. (Scooped-out sugar may be used to mold smaller shapes.) Set the sugar form, rounded side down, back on the cardboard to dry about three or four hours—or dry about 20 minutes in a 200°F oven.

Hollow the cut-off half-form the same way. First remove the cut-off portion with a spatula, then hold the form in your palm and scoop out the sugar, leaving a window opening. Smooth edge of window with your finger and dry thoroughly on cardboard, window side up. Use the same procedure to hollow out the other ornaments.

**Make cute trims to
put inside the hollow forms**

There's no limit to the decor you can set inside your hollow forms. Bake tiny gingerbread people. Make a little tree by piping a spiral cone shape with tube 16 and trim it with tube 3 balls. Or cover a 2″ wax paper cone with tube 65 leaves, starting at bottom. Figure-pipe a snowman with tube 5. Use royal icing for all.

Make an elf out of miniature and regular-size marshmallows, painted with thinned royal icing and put together with toothpicks. Give him a tube 32 hat. Use marshmallows for the portraits of Santa and his bride. Pipe a cluster of royal icing holly leaves.

A beautiful standing ornament is made from a 5″ hollow egg, filled with red roses on wire stems. The base is sugar-molded from a shot glass.

**How to put
everything together**

Royal icing is the glue used to assemble the panorama eggs. Let's use the snowman ball as an example. Pipe a generous mound of icing just behind the window of the half-ball. Set the snowman on it, and slightly behind him, the tree. Prop with crumpled foil to dry.

Twist a 1½″ piece of wire into a loop, ends spread out, as shown. Attach to rim of other half ball with icing. Pipe a line of icing around the entire rim and gently press the window half of the egg on it. Dry thoroughly.

*Attach wire loop to
ornament with royal icing*

Decorating with royal icing is the most fun. Pipe zigzag, leaf or bead borders around the windows and to cover the seams. Santa and Mrs. Santa place markers are simply hollow eggs set on bases made of rolled 1¼″ strips of colored paper. Pipe the hair and features, then add the name on the base. The children will be thrilled. The candy baskets are 4½″ hollow half-balls. Make a hole on opposite sides near the top with a heated ice pick. Curve an 8″ length of stiff wire into a handle, hook the ends and insert in the holes. Wind ribbon over the handles, pipe a zigzag base, add other trim and finish with bows at bottom of handles.

For a touch of sparkle, spray the completed trims with clear acrylic, then sprinkle on edible glitter. Caution: sprayed pieces are not edible. Thread ribbon or cord through the wire loops to hang the tree ornaments. Don't they look jolly on the branches?

CHAPTER EIGHT

Figure piping creates three-dimensional forms in icing

This technique produces enchanting cake trims as if by magic by using careful pressure control. The playful figures you'll pipe will appeal especially to children—and the technique is really easy. If you can pipe a simple ball, you'll be able to create many cute figures.

The stick figure method is easiest to start with

You don't need to be an artist to draw a simple stick figure in icing, then fill it in to achieve a rounded sculptural figure in high relief. Let's start with a jolly clown, always a favorite with youngsters.

1. Make a half-recipe of Figure Piping Icing (page 23) for this practice. Start your practice immediately, for this icing does not hold well. On the back of a cookie sheet, draw a stick figure with tube 3. This one is about 4" high from top of head to toe.

2. Use tube 10 to fill in the body. Start at the base, holding tube at a 45° angle and about ⅛" above the surface. Squeeze to press out a large mound, lifting tube as the icing builds up. Move slowly forward, relaxing pressure slightly to form a pear shape. The tip of the tube should always be buried. Stop pressure *before* pulling away.

Hold tube 10 straight up to pipe a ball for head. Let icing mound up as you lift tube, keeping tip buried. Stop pressure completely, pull away.

Insert the same tube into the body to pipe arms and legs. Hold tube slightly above the surface at a 45° angle, and let icing build up as you move slowly along, applying even pressure.

Change to tube 5 to pipe a ball for hand, holding tube straight up above surface. Stick tube in side of ball and use light pressure to pull out the thumb. Use tube 5 again to pipe the feet, starting with a ball at toe, then relaxing pressure as you move back to heel.

3. Add the finishing touches to give the clown personality. Pipe three ball buttons on his suit with tube 5. Pipe features and spiky hair with tube 3, then add ruffles with tube 101. Touch wide end of tube to surface, narrow end straight out, apply even pressure and jiggle your hand as you move. Your cute clown is complete!

Draw the figure with tube 3, then fill in with tubes 5 and 10. Tube 101 pipes ruffles

Pipe clowns to frolic on a birthday cake

The lucky birthday child will always remember this spirited cake!

1. Bake and fill a two-layer 9" x 13" sheet cake. Swirl boiled icing (page 23) over the surface, then pipe a colorful ball border with tube 7. Pipe tube 3 stick figures for the three clowns, doing center clown first. Fill in the clowns as described above.

2. Mark an arc with a toothpick above clowns' heads and use it as a guide to pipe six balloons with tube 7. Connect balloons to hands with tube 1 string. Pipe balls for clowns to kick and stand on with tube 7. Print "HAPPY BIRTHDAY" with tube 3, and child's name on balloons with tube 1. Insert candles in holders and light up the scene. Serves 24.

Simple trims set off the colorful clowns

109

Upright figure piping is also based on pressure control

You'll enjoy this form of figure piping even more than the stick figure method! By following correct techniques you can pipe upright, completely three-dimensional realistic figures.

Good control of your pressure is essential for piping these upright figures—in fact this method is sometimes called "pressure formation" piping. So review pages 33 through 35 for pressure control practice.

Upright figures may be piped directly on the cake, or off the cake on a surface covered with wax paper. After they're thoroughly dry, they may be placed on the cake. Attach wax paper to the back of a cookie sheet with a few lines of icing to practice eggs, then chicks, in a nest.

Pipe a nest filled with Easter eggs

1. Make a half-recipe of Figure Piping Icing for this practice. Mark a 2" circle on the wax paper by tracing a 2" cookie cutter. Hold tube 10 straight up, slightly above surface, and use even pressure to pipe the circle. Keep tip of tube buried in the icing. When circle is complete, stop pressure and pull away. Cover the circle with short tube 3 strings to give a straw-like effect.

2. Fill the nest with tube 5 eggs. Set tube in nest, held almost straight up about ⅛" above surface. Squeeze evenly to let icing build up, lifting tube along with it. When an oval shape has been achieved, stop pressure, then lift off. Repeat until nest is full.

Pipe a cute baby chick in a nest

1. Use Figure Piping Icing as before to pipe the nest on a wax paper-covered surface.

2. Now pipe the baby chick. Hold tube 7 at a 45° angle, almost touching inside of nest at the front. Squeeze heavily to form the body, moving tube back as it builds up. Decrease pressure as you approach the tail, moving tube back and up. Stop pressure, then pull off for pointed tail.

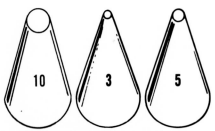

Three tubes pipe eggs in a nest

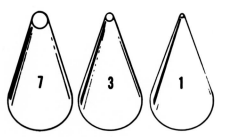

Pipe a baby chick in the nest

Hold tube straight up, tuck into front of body, and use heavy pressure to form a ball for head, lifting tube as it forms. Stop pressure completely, then move away.

For wings, change to tube 3. Tuck tube into side of body, squeeze heavily, then relax pressure, stop completely and move away to form pointed tip. This is a similar technique to piping a shell.

3. Use tube 1 to finish the chick. Pull out a tiny leg, then add 3 strokes for claws. Set tube against front of head and pull out lower beak, then upper beak. Add two blue dots for eyes. Your finished chick looks almost real enough to chirp!

Everything about this Easter cake sings spring!

Bright colors, dainty flowers and cheerful chicks make a happy Easter centerpiece to display with pride.

1. Do trims in advance. Pipe nests, eggs and chicks on wax paper as shown on opposite page and dry thoroughly, at least 24 hours. Pipe drop flowers in bright royal icing with tube 225 and add tube 2 dots for centers. Dry thoroughly.

2. Bake and chill a two-layer 10" round lower tier, each layer about 2" high. Bake the two-layer top tier in 6" petal-shaped pans, each layer about 1½" high. (You may use 6" round pans, if you prefer.) Fill and ice smoothly in buttercream. Divide lower tier into eighths and mark at base of tier. Divide each division into halves for a total of 16 marks. If you are using 6" round pans for top tier, divide tier into eighths and mark at base. Place 10" tier on cake board or serving tray, then set 6" tier on top of it, toward rear.

3. Pipe tube 21 garlands at base of 10" tier from mark to mark. Frame each garland with tube 13 zigzags, then add a star where frames meet. Pipe a tube 2 spray of stems above every other garland and attach flowers by piping a dot of icing on back of each, then pressing to cake side. Finish with tube 65 leaves. Add a tube 19 shell border at top of tier.

Use tube 19 to pipe a shell border at base of 6" tier. Using petal shape as guide, pipe tube 2 stems on side of cake. (Or use marks if tier is round.) Attach flowers and pipe tube 65 leaves. Do top shell border with tube 13.

4. Set nests on cake and trim with a few more flowers and leaves. Serve this pretty spring tableau to 20—the nests are a bonus for the children.

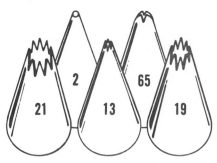

Pipe the drop flowers in advance

Star tubes border the cake

Top a birthday cake with his favorite toy

Here's just the cutest cake ever created to celebrate a toddler's birthday!
Chubby pastel teddy bears express the birthday greeting and there's a
little cake topped by a teddy for each guest. Pipe the bears ahead of
time—then decorating the cakes is a breeze.

Toothpicks give support to the teddy bears

Since these upright figures are quite large, toothpicks inserted in the
bodies help them hold their upright form.

1. Cover the back of a cookie sheet with wax paper by piping a few lines
of icing on it, then pressing on the paper. Fit a decorating cone with tube
1A and fill with Figure Piping Icing. Hold the cone straight up, slightly
above surface and use heavy pressure to pipe the cone-shaped body.
Raise the tube as the body builds up, relaxing pressure as you approach
the top. Body should be about 1¾" high. Stop pressure before moving
away. Immediately insert a toothpick, moistened with water.

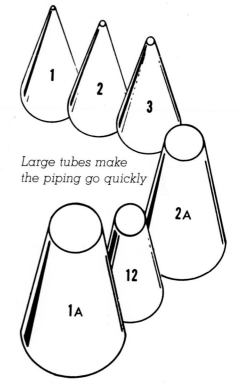

*Large tubes make
the piping go quickly*

Use tube 2A to pipe the legs. Insert tube into body and exert even
pressure, moving out as the form builds up. Stop pressure, then move
away. Hind legs are about ¾" long.

Pipe a tube 12 ball for head, then poke tube 3 into ball and pipe the
bear's nose. Use the same tube to pipe half-circle ears.

2. Pipe two balls with tube 2 for eyes, then top with tube 1 dots of blue
piping gel. Pipe a red piping gel heart at the end of the nose by joining
two tube 1 shell shapes. Finish this loveable little pet by attaching a
jaunty drop flower with a dot of icing. Dry at least 24 hours.

Decorate the birthday cake

1. Make lots of tube 225 drop flowers in royal icing. Pipe centers with
tube 2 and dry. See directions on page 94.

2. Bake a two-layer 10" round cake, each layer about 2" high. Bake a 2"
high sheet cake, too, for the guests' take-home treats. Chill, then fill and
ice the round cake with white buttercream. Divide cake side into twelfths
and mark at top edge with a toothpick. (See page 42.)

Continued on next page

Make a paper pattern for the birthday greeting. First fold a 10" circle into quarters to determine center. Unfold and print letters about 1½" in from edge. All verticals should point toward center. Transfer pattern to cake top by pricking through with a pin. Place cake on serving tray.

3. Circle the base of the cake with tube 19 rosettes. Use tube 2 to drop string guidelines for garlands from mark to mark on top edge of cake, then do lettering with the same tube. Pipe a tube 16 top shell border. Make the garlands by massing flowers to follow guidelines, attaching each with a dot of icing. Finish with tube 65 ruffled leaves. This will serve 14 delighted guests.

Decorate the individual cakes

1. Cut the chilled sheet cake into 2" squares and ice smoothly with tinted buttercream. Small cakes like these are most easily iced by spearing the bottom with a fork, and turning the fork as you ice each side. Any roughness at corners will be hidden by the border. Reserve two cakes to set on the birthday cake and place the others on small doilies.

2. Do lettering on all cakes with tube 2. Pipe shell borders with tube 13. Attach flower trims with dots of icing and garnish with tube 65 leaves.

Arrange two cake squares on top of the birthday cake and push in tall tapers behind them. Set the teddy bears on all the cakes and call the children to the table. Listen to their cries of delight! *Caution:* warn the guests that toothpicks are inside the piped teddy bears.

*Simple borders trim
the small cakes*

*Each guest will
take his own pet home*

114

CHAPTER NINE

The Color Flow technique lets you draw in icing

Yes, you can really put a colored line drawing of almost any subject on a cake! All it takes is a special icing and a sure hand. Turn the page to learn how to create this plaque with the look of fine porcelain—and see the other uses of this amazing technique. You can curve Color Flow, make it stand upright and reproduce club emblems and designs.

1. Tape pattern to a rigid surface, tape wax paper smoothly over it and then do outline with tube 2.

2. Fill in the design with thinned icing, using a cone with a cut tip. Work steadily so no crust lines will show on completed work.

3. The finished design has the sheen of fine porcelain!

A beautiful cake-top plaque in the Color Flow Technique

Plaques or other decorations made with this technique can be done even months ahead and carefully stored—then a distinctive cake can be decorated in a hurry. You'll be inspired to create your own original pieces, using any favorite picture, cartoon or emblem. Some Color Flow designs are so beautiful they've been framed for lovely wall decor!

COLOR FLOW ICING

>   1 pound confectioners' sugar
>   2 level tablespoons Color Flow mix
>   3 ounces water

Combine sugar and Color Flow mix, then add water. Set electric mixer at low speed and mix for five minutes. Too high a speed will beat air into the icing and the finished work may have bubbles. Use at once and keep bowl covered with a damp cloth while working—icing dries quickly.

First outline the design

Tape the pattern from the Appendix (starting on page 162) to a piece of glass, plexiglass or stiff cardboard. Tape wax paper smoothly over the pattern. Remove a small portion of the icing and tint a light green for this graduation plaque. Fill a small decorating cone fitted with tube 2 and outline the design, keeping lines as smooth as possible. If an icing line is a little out of place, nudge it into position with a damp artist's brush. If your fill-in work is done in a similar color, as on this plaque, you need dry the outline only a few minutes until icing crusts. If you are using a much deeper, or very contrasting color for outlining, dry thoroughly, about an hour, so color will not bleed into fill-in work.

Fill in the areas with thinned icing

To speed your work, do all sections of the same hue at one time. First thin the icing. Place a portion from the original batch in a small bowl and tint medium green. Stir in water, a few drops at a time—*never beat*. To test for proper consistency, let a spoonful of icing drop back into bowl. If it disappears at the count of ten, icing will be just right.

Fill a decorating cone *just half full* (more and icing may back up and drip on design). If you need more than this amount to fill in an area, have a second cone filled and ready. Cut a small opening at the tip of the cone. A tube is never used as it might break the delicate outline.

Starting just inside the outline of a letter, press out the icing gently, letting it flow by itself to touch outline. Then fill in entire area quickly before icing crusts. If bubbles appear, prick with a pin. Now do the fill-in for the other colored areas with thinned icing—first blue for the ribbon, then white for diploma and last, light green for the background.

Dry the completed design thoroughly

Drying times vary according to the humidity of your house, but allow at least 48 hours. To speed drying time, place the design under a heat lamp, hung about two feet above the design. (If distance is closer, design may bubble.) Dry under the lamp for two hours, then complete drying without lamp for about twelve hours. This gives a higher gloss.

Remove dried design from wax paper

With a sharp knife, cut taped edges of wax paper. Place a piece of soft foam over the design, then cover it with a piece of glass, plexiglass or stiff cardboard. Turn this "sandwich" over and the design will be upside down. Carefully peel away the wax paper. Your completed plaque may be stored almost indefinitely, carefully boxed and covered to protect from dust and light. To place it on a lovely cake, see page 121.

Make curved petals in Color Flow for a perfect poinsettia

Yes, you can curve Color Flow pieces! Review the basic method on the opposite page, then create these amazingly life-like poinsettias.

1. Transfer the pattern from the Appendix (starting page on page 162) to a piece of heavy paper or light cardboard. Cut out and trace it eight times on a piece of paper, leaving about 2" between each petal shape. Tape this pattern to a rigid surface. Attach a small square of wax paper over each petal shape with a few dots of icing.

2. Fit a cone with tube 2 and fill with Color Flow icing for outlining. Fill another cone half full with thinned icing and cut the tip. Outline a petal with the first cone and immediately fill in with the thinned icing. Lift paper square, with petal, to a Flower Former to dry. Dry four petals within a former and four petals on outside of a former.

3. Assemble the flower. Pipe a mound of green royal icing on wax paper with tube 9. Insert pointed ends of petals into mound, alternating up-curved and down-curved petals. Cover the mound with a cluster of tube 3 green dots. Top each green dot with a yellow, then a red dot, piped with tube 1. Dry thoroughly.

The loveliest Christmas cake is trimmed with poinsettias

1. Make twelve Color Flow poinsettias as described above. Pipe 30 holly leaves in royal icing as shown on page 104, and dry thoroughly.

2. Bake and fill a two-layer, 10" round cake. Ice smoothly with white buttercream. Divide cake side into sixths and mark at top edge and base. Place cake on serving tray or cake board. *Note:* flat surface of tray on which cake rests must measure at least 14".

3. Do all borders with tube 19. At base of cake, pipe a zigzag garland against cake side from mark to mark. Pipe a second garland on cake tray, just below first garland. Pipe a fleur-de-lis between each set of garlands. Pipe garlands on cake side at top edge from mark to mark, then pipe garlands on top of cake to cover edge.

Pipe mounds of icing with tube 19, and gently press in leaves and poinsettias. Use the picture as a guide.

Fluffy borders are piped with just one tube

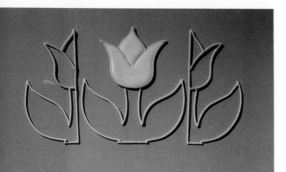

Outline and fill in front

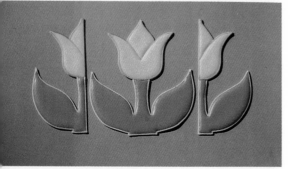

Dry, outline and fill in back

Assemble the tulip

Color Flow can make a tulip bloom

Use this versatile technique to create upright, three-dimensional trims. The basic method makes the forms, then they are assembled into the charming stylized flowers.

Outline and fill in the pieces

Review page 116 for the basic Color Flow technique. Each tulip is constructed of two half-flower and one full flower shape. Tape the patterns from the Appendix (starting on page 162) to stiff board, glass or plexiglass. Outline the petals with tube 2 and orange Color Flow icing, the stem and leaf areas with yellow icing and the same tube. Since the thinned icings used for filling in are of very constrasting colors, allow the outline to dry about an hour before flowing the areas.

Make sure the pieces are completely dry before turning over and carefully peeling off the wax paper.

Turn pieces over to outline and fill in backs

Since these little flowers are three-dimensional and will be seen from all angles, the backs must be as finished-looking as the fronts. When you are sure the pieces are completely dry, turn them over and outline and fill in the backs, just as you did the fronts. (If pieces have not dried thoroughly, the thinned icing used for fill-in on the back may soften the front.) Dry thoroughly again.

Assemble the flowers

It's fun and very easy to put the tulips together. First cut 2" thick styrofoam into 2" squares to use as supports. (Small cardboard boxes will serve, too.) Pipe a line of unthinned Color Flow icing with tube 2 along the straight edge of a half-flower. Press to the center of the full flower and prop with three styrofoam blocks. Pipe a line of icing on straight edge of second half-flower and press to other side of full flower. Prop completed flower with a fourth block and let dry thoroughly. The finished flower will stand upright and perky by itself.

Plant the tulips in pots

Here's a centerpiece as fresh as springtime that will last all year! We grouped our potted tulips on a tray to center the table, but you could use one to mark each guest's place.

1. Make four Color Flow tulips as described above. Use the brilliant colors of the natural flowers. Assemble and dry.

2. Sugar mold the pots according to directions on page 105. We used a Small Wonder Mold pan as a mold and cut about ¾" off the small end with a taut thread to give them stability, but you can use any container with a top diameter of about 3½". Dry the pots thoroughly, then paint with thinned royal icing.

3. Set the pots on wax paper to decorate with royal icing. Pipe inverted shells around base with tube 19, then add stars. Pipe a zigzag on side with tube 16. Heap icing on top and pull up into points with a small spatula, then add a tube 13 top zigzag border.

While icing is still wet, gently press an assembled tulip into pot. Bring these tulips out anytime you want to make the table look special, or when you'd like to think spring!

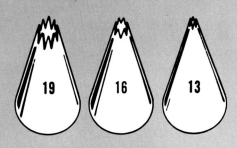

Decorate the pots simply
with royal icing
and three star tubes.
They'll last indefinitely

Here's a happy cake to usher in the Fourth

Patriotic colors, bright sugar stars and a showy Color Flow plaque make this an outstanding celebration cake. Serve it on the porch or patio after a glorious summer day.

1. First make the plaque, as far ahead of time as you like. Page 116 tells how. Do all outlining in red icing. Since the thinned icing used for fill-in is sharply contrasting, let the outline dry for about an hour before flowing in the areas. When plaque is finished and dry, remove from wax paper and edge the circle area with tube 3 royal icing dots.

Use candy molds and the method on page 105 to form the sugar stars. You'll need 16. To make them sparkle, sprinkle with edible glitter as soon as they come out of the molds.

2. Bake two 10" round cake layers, each about 2" high. Chill, then fill and ice with buttercream. Divide cake side into sixteenths and mark at top edge and about 1" up from base. Set cake on serving tray.

3. Pipe a tube 13 shell border around base of cake. Now pipe tube 104 curves from mark to mark with blue icing. Hold wide end of tube against cake, narrow end flaring out. Just above it, pipe a second row of curves in red icing. Drop red strings from mark to mark on top edge of cake with tube 2. Drop a row of blue strings below them, then finish top edge with tube 19 shells. Pipe a small mound of icing on the back of each star, then press to side of cake.

Set six flat sugar cubes in a 5" circle on top of cake. Attach each by piping a dot of icing on back. Just before serving time, set the plaque on the sugar cubes. Simply lift it off before cutting the cake into 14 servings.

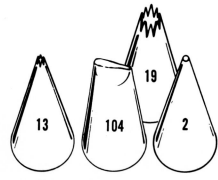

Four tubes and brightly tinted icing trim a festive cake

Honor the graduate with a distinctive cake

You've something to be proud of—so show it by decorating this center-piece cake! The Color Flow plaque spells out your good wishes, and the leafy green trim expresses bright hope for the years ahead.

1. Make the Color Flow plaque just as directed on page 116. You can do this weeks ahead of time so the work goes very quickly on decorating day. Dry thoroughly and peel off wax paper.

2. Bake a two-layer 10" round cake in the graduate's favorite flavor, each layer about 2" high. Chill the layers, then fill and ice smoothly with white buttercream. Divide cake side into ninths and mark about 1" up from base. Make a mark half-way between each division for a total division of 18. Place on serving tray.

3. Carefully center the plaque on cake top. Do this by placing six flat sugar cubes in a 7" circle on top of cake as described on facing page, and setting the plaque on the cubes. Or pipe a mound of icing in the center of the cake, and then six mounds of icing within a 7" circle. Set plaque on mounds. Border the plaque with tube 13 shells.

4. Pipe a tube 13 zigzag border at base of cake. Swing tube 104 curves from mark to mark above it, holding wide end of tube against cake, narrow end pointing out. Now pipe a tube 1 curving vine on cake side and pull out short stems from it. Pipe ruffled, pointed leaves with tube 67. Finish the cake with a tube 19 shell border at top.

This tribute to your graduate serves 14 party guests. To serve, slide a knife under the plaque, place it on a cake circle and present it to the graduate as a memento of the occasion.

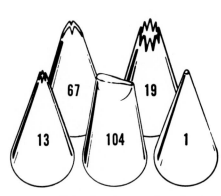

A leafy vine and swinging curves trim the cake side, star tube borders edge the cake

CHAPTER TEN

Short-cut, show-off cakes

Very little time but want a really stunning cake? Look through this chapter. Here are some of the prettiest cakes you could make—and every one can be done in a hurry. Some are gaily informal to bring to a picnic, take to a bake sale, send to school. Others are splendid enough to center a formal dinner table or even grace an intimate wedding reception. It's a versatile group!

Learn the quick tricks of trimming a cake with flowers, fresh fruit or candy. See how cookie cutters or a decorating comb can pattern a cake in a trice. You'll be glad you did, the next time you want a beautiful cake in next-to-no-time.

A crown of fresh flowers glorifies a ring cake

Have you ever seen a more striking centerpiece? The colorful flowers make it beautiful enough to grace the table at your nicest dinner party, then do double duty as dessert. Let the flowers dictate the tint of the icing. We used brilliant zinnias and golden statice set off by a yellow cake, but any flowers of small-to-medium size from your garden or the florist are lovely.

Before beginning, decide on the container for the flowers. Our cake was baked in an 11" ring mold, and a small white plastic footed bowl fit the center opening perfectly. You may decide on a dessert or cereal bowl—just be sure it fits easily into the hole in the cake.

1. Bake the cake. Your favorite rich pound cake batter is ideal for a ring mold. Chill for an hour or so while you mix the icing and arrange the flowers. Ice the chilled cake with a thin coating of white buttercream, and set it on a rack over a cookie sheet. Make a recipe of Quick Poured Fondant, page 23, (it takes just a few moments) and pour it over the cake, touching up any uncovered spots with a spatula. Let the fondant set, then transfer the cake to a serving tray. Pipe a simple tube 32 shell border around the base.

2. Arrange the flowers. You may do this in the morning, and refrigerate, or just before the party. A fast way to a beautiful, lasting floral arrangement is to first pack the container with Oasis, obtained from your florist. Soak the Oasis well with water, then insert the flower stems. They will stay firmly in position. Be sure the arrangement is perfect from every point of view—it will be the center of attention. Set the bowl in the opening of the cake and bring it to the table. At serving time, remove the bowl of flowers and present it to the guest of honor. This 11" ring cake serves twelve, generously.

The fondant coating keeps the cake moist and fresh for a long time–so you can make it ahead, if you like.

A shell border finishes the cake

Cookie cutters make cute cake designs

Here are the perfect cakes to give away! Bake them from your favorite mix or recipe in disposable foil pans, then ice with luscious buttercream. Easy serving, easy carrying and no pans to wash or return—just delighted thanks!

What makes these cakes real conversation pieces are their colorful patterns. They look so intricate and attractive no one will ever believe that cookie cutters pressed into the icing created the designs.

Pack a sunny circle cake for a picnic . . .

and watch them "ooh!" and "ah!" when you bring it out. You'll need a foil pan (ours is 11½" x 9", but you can adjust the design for a different size), 4", 2" and 1½" round cutters and tube 16 for decorating.

1. Bake and cool the cake. Make a half-recipe of the Snow-white Buttercream on page 22, and tint it a soft yellow. Swirl it over the cake, then divide remaining icing into three parts. Tint one part a deeper yellow by adding a speck of orange, add more orange to the second part, and add red to the third part for a brilliant scarlet.

2. Lightly press the 4" cutter in the center of the cake. Center the circle with a 2" cutter, then press the same cutter on all four sides of the 4" circle, just touching it. Complete the design by filling in with the 1½" cutter as picture shows. Pipe tube 16 stars right over the marked design, starting with deep yellow icing, then red and finally orange. Add an orange zigzag border, then complete the picture with rosettes within the circles and fleurs-de-lis surrounding them. A minor masterpiece!

Take a sweet cake to the bake sale . . .

it will be the first one sold! Bake and cool the cake in a foil pan approximately 11½" x 9". You'll need heart cutters, about 4" and 1½", tube 16 for decorating and tube 3 for the script.

1. Make a half-recipe of Snow-white Buttercream, page 22, and tint it a delicate pink. Swirl over the cake. Tint remaining icing a deeper pink.

2. Lightly press the 4" cutter in the center of the cake and slightly to one end. Press the small heart cutter at the point and indentation of the large heart. Fill in design by pressing the small cutter five times around each side of the large heart, then press a small heart in each corner of the cake. Outline all marked small hearts with curved elongated shells in deep pink, then add a shell border. Write your message in the center of the large heart with tube 3.

Now add red color to remaining icing and outline the large heart with tube 16 stars. Trim the small hearts with red stars and pipe a shell and two stars at the base of the large design. Don't wait for Valentine's Day to make this charmer—love is always in season!

Send a friendly cake to school . . .

or just have an impromptu party for the neighborhood youngsters. Bake a cake in a foil pan, make a half-recipe of buttercream and get out a round cutter about 2½" in diameter and a 2½" or 3" heart cutter.

1. Ice the cake top in white, then tint remaining icing in bright colors. Press the round cutter into the icing to form an arc of four circles. Press the heart cutter below them.

2. Pipe a scalloped border and trim each point with a star. Pipe a greeting within the heart, then outline it with two curved elongated shells. The faces are the most fun! Eyes and noses are rosettes, smiles and chubby chins are curves, coiffures are whatever you dream up!

Now that you've seen these quick crowd-pleasers, get out your cookie cutters and make a few magic cake designs of your own. You might want to start by tracing the cutters on a pan-size sheet of paper.

Pipe circles of color on a cake top

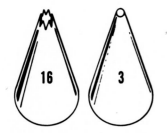

Pink hearts trim a love cake

Smiling faces say "hello!"

Directions for the quick-to-do "ice cream cones" on page 127

A cascade of pink azaleas

Three rosy heart-shaped tiers, simple one-tube borders, a dainty cupid ornament and a few fresh flowers combine to make a cake lovely enough for a bride's small reception—but you can turn it out in less than an hour! Of course you can serve this cake on other occasions too—an anniversary, an elegant luncheon, or serve it at a party to announce an engagement.

We baked the tiers in mini-heart pans, 5", 7½" and 9", using two cake mixes. If you would like a larger cake, bake two-layer tiers in 6", 9" and 12" heart-shaped pans.

1. Bake and chill the two-layer tiers. Set each on a plastic-wrapped cake base, cut to size, for ease in separating for serving. (See page 24.)

If you have chosen to use the larger pans, insert dowels in the two lower tiers for support, as described on page 146. Fill and ice the tiers with buttercream, then assemble on a serving tray, or, as the picture shows, a ruffle-edged cake board.

2. The borders are easy but effective. Use tube 9 to pipe a heart at the point of the base of the bottom tier. Do this by piping two shell shapes, close together. Now surround the base with neat balls. Do the same at the top edge of the tier, piping a heart, then a few balls, then another heart as picture shows. Border the top two tiers in the same way.

3. The secret of the lasting fresh flower cascade is a set of small hollow tubes called Flower Spikes. Insert the pointed end of one in the lowest tier at a slanted angle. Use two for the middle tier and one on the top of highest tier. Fill the spikes with water, using an eye dropper, then arrange blossoms in spikes. Any favorite small flower is suitable. Set the little cherub fountain ornament on top with a final blossom. Baked in mini-tier pans, this dainty creation will serve 42 wedding-size pieces.

Just one big tube makes decorating fast and easy

"Ice cream cones" thrill the children

It's lucky these treats are so quick to make—once you send a tray of them to class there'll be calls for more! They're pretty, easy to serve, neat and sweet to eat! Perfect school-time treats!

Here's how to do it. Fill cup-shaped ice cream cones about three-quarters full with your favorite cake batter. Set on a cookie sheet and bake about 30 minutes in a pre-heated 325°F oven, or until done. Use buttercream or Egg White Boiled Icing (pages 22, 23) for the "ice cream." Tint in varied pastels and swirl it on in a spiral cone shape, holding tube 4B straight up. Be prepared to serve seconds!

Create sculptured texture in just a few minutes

The two little cakes at left look extra fancy because the icing is given an interesting sculptured effect with a simple tool, the decorating comb. The plastic comb is shaped like a ruler or triangle with serrated edges. They're washable and very inexpensive, but you might like to make your own of stiff cardboard, about 4" x 6". Along the 6" side, make a mark every ¼". Draw a light line ¼" down from the marked edge. With a sharp knife (an X-acto is best), zigzag the edge down to the line so the points are ½" apart.

Give a square cake a candy bouquet

1. Bake a two-layer 8" square cake, about 3" high. Fill the chilled layers and give them the usual thin coating of icing (page 25). Let this set a short time, then ice the top smoothly in buttercream. Swirl a contrasting icing on the sides, using plenty for a thick coating.

Immediately, lightly press the decorating comb against the side of the cake and use an up-and-down, zigzag motion to texture the icing. Don't worry about any roughness at edges. This will be covered by borders. Allow icing to set, then transfer cake to serving tray.

2. Pipe a puffy shell border at base with tube 22. Use tube 18 for shell border at top. The little nosegay is easy to make. Insert toothpicks into about a dozen gumdrops and stick into center of cake. Slice some green gumdrops for leaves and circle the bouquet. Serves twelve.

Wreath a round cake with flowers

The lavish continental look of this cake is achieved with a decorating comb and three tints of icing. You'll be glad you saved your practice drop flowers to form the pretty border.

1. Bake a two-layer 8" round cake about 4" high. Fill, then give the cake a thin crumb coat of white buttercream. (You'll need a half-recipe of Snow-white Buttercream to do this cake.) Leave one-third of the remaining icing untinted, and tint the remainder a delicate pink. Tint half of this pink icing a deep pink.

2. Heap white icing on top of cake, spread to cover and run the decorating comb in deep curves across it. The ombre effect on the sides is easy to do. Spread deep pink icing thickly on the lower half of the side. On the top half of the side spread light pink icing. Hold the decorating comb against the side and move up and down in curves for the scallop shapes. The two tints of pink will blend prettily.

Add tube 22 puffy shells at base. Press about 20 made-ahead drop flowers around the top edge. Ours were made with tube 190, but any rather large drop flower is fine. Tint a little buttercream green and surround the flowers with tube 67 leaves. This dainty treat serves ten.

Turn a dessert tray into a garden

Give an everyday dinner a festive finale by bringing in scoops of ice cream crowned with roses! Nothing could be quicker or easier. Make the ice cream balls ahead, if you like, and store in the freezer.

Go through your store of made-ahead flowers and pick out the ones you want to use. Royal icing flowers are fine—the ice cream will tend to soften them. Frozen buttercream flowers are just as good.

Just before serving, place the ice cream balls in serving dishes. Pipe a little mound of buttercream on the back of a flower, press it on the ice cream ball, then add a few tube 67 green leaves. Wouldn't these be beautiful to serve with the wedding cake at a bridal reception?

The serrated edge of a decorating comb patterns the icing

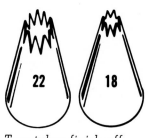

Two tubes finish off a pretty square cake

Just one border and piped leaves complete a round cake

Add leaves to made-ahead flowers

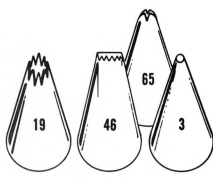

Form a rosebud with tube 19, a draped border with tube 46

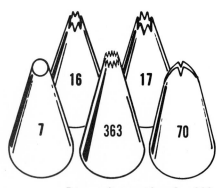

Pipe tulips with tube 363, add long leaves with tube 70

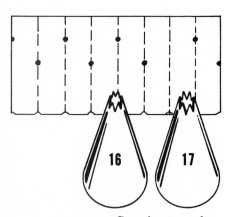

Simple star tubes create a daisy garden

Trim summery cakes with fast-growing flowers

Everyone loves flowers, and loves to see them on a cake, whatever the season. But decorators know that most icing flowers must be piped ahead of time and dried or frozen. The flowers on these three blooming cakes are exceptions. They're piped in buttercream right on the cake, they're easy and fast to do, and they're beautiful! The next time you want a colorful, flowery cake in a hurry, let one of these beauties inspire you!

Rosebuds ring a pretty pink cake

Just a little twirl of tube 19 makes a very realistic rosebud. Pipe a garland of them on this feminine cake.

1. Bake a two-layer, 8″ round cake, about 4″ high. Chill, fill and ice smoothly with pink buttercream. Trace the pattern in the Appendix, starting on page 162, on the cake top. Using outer curves of marked cake top pattern as guide, make ten marks on side of cake, about 1″ up from base. Place cake on serving tray.

2. Circle the base of the cake with tube 19 shells. Tint remaining pink icing a deeper pink and use to pipe the tube 46 swag border. Starting at one marked point, jiggle your hand down-and-up twice, then curve to next point. Repeat around cake. Use tube 3 to pipe the curving pattern on top of cake. Pipe a tube 19 rosette, exactly as shown on page 32, at deepest point of each curve. Complete the rosebud garland by piping three tube 65 leaves on each short stem. This flowery treat serves ten.

Bright tulips bloom on a sunny square

Tinted icing and tube 363 create the rounded form of a tulip in three quick motions. Don't wait for spring to pipe them on a cake!

1. Bake a two-layer, 8″ square cake, 4″ high. Chill, fill and ice with buttercream. Place on cake stand. Make a mark at center of cake top, and one in the center of each side at base of cake.

2. With tube 7, draw a long stem from center of cake top straight down to center mark at base. Pipe a shorter curved stem on either side of it on cake side. Using center marks as guides, pipe three short stems on remaining three sides of cake.

The tulips are quickly piped. At end of stem on cake top, pipe an outward curving shell with tube 363, then one right beside it curving in opposite direction. Pipe a center shell on top of these two—you've made a tulip! Pipe three tulips on each side of cake, then add long tube 70 leaves. Finish with shell borders, tube 17 at base, tube 16 at top. A quick-to-do cake tht serves twelve.

Pipe a daisy patch on a bright little cake

It's just the right size to brighten a family dinner or to bring as a cheer-up gift to a friend. Simple shells form the colorful daisies.

1. Bake an 8″ x 2″ square cake and cut in half. Chill, fill and stack the two halves, then ice with buttercream or boiled icing (page 23).

2. Make a pattern for the cake sides so daisies grow in orderly rows. Cut a 4″ strip of paper the exact length of the long side of cake. Fold in eighths, then cut a notch in folded pattern near the bottom on both sides, another 3″ up from base on one side, 1¾″ up from base on other side. Page 42 shows the easy method. Open pattern, pin to cake side and mark notches with a toothpick. Use half the pattern to mark short sides.

3. Pipe tube 16 stems from marks to base of cake. Let one stem rise to top edge of cake as picture shows. For the daisies, pipe a circle of tube 17 shells, their tails joining at the top of the stems. With the same tube, pipe a rosette in the center. Trim the flowers with tube 16 leaves and add a tube 16 shell border at base. Slices neatly into eight 1″ pieces.

Sparkling glazed fruits
shimmer like jewels on a hurry-up cake

This beautiful cake will turn a backyard barbecue into an elegant al fresco feast, star at a sweet table at a bridal reception, or be the bright finale of a festive dinner. It's very quick and easy to produce—make the cake the day before or morning of the party, then just before serving time, glaze the fruit and arrange on the cake. Don't attempt to glaze the fruit much ahead of time—the fruit acids will eat into the glittering glaze rather quickly and detract from the appearance of the cake.

Prepare the cake ahead of time

Bake and fill a 9″ or 10″ two-layer cake. Chill, then swirl on boiled icing (page 23), and place on serving tray. Boiled icing, being grease-free, makes the best base for glazed fruit.

Glaze the fresh fruits

Select perfect small fruits, strawberries, seedless grapes or cherries. Carefully wash and dry them, refrigerate until about an hour before serving time, then prepare the glaze.

CARAMEL GLAZE
    2 cups granulated sugar
    2/3 cups water
    ¼ teaspoon of cream of tartar

Mix the sugar, water and cream of tartar together in a heavy pan. Bring to a boil over high heat, stirring constantly. When it begins to boil, stop stirring and cook to 305°F. Remove from heat and set pan in a bowl of hot water while dipping fruit—the glaze hardens very quickly. Caution: mixture is extremely hot. Be sure to keep a bowl of cold water nearby in case you accidently drip some of the glaze on your hand.

Insert a cocktail pick into each piece of fruit and pat dry again. (A small cluster of grapes may be held by the stem.) Quickly dip into glaze and set on an oiled tray to harden, just a few minutes. Arrange in clusters on top and side of cake. As an added touch, we tucked in washed ivy leaves. Serve to 14, giving each guest a cluster of fruit with the cake.

These glazed fruits are a special treat. The crackling clear sugar coating gives a delicious taste and crunch to the fresh fruit.

CHAPTER ELEVEN

Lettering and script
add a personal touch

A cake always means more when there's a special message and a name piped on it with icing. Of course, every birthday cake must have its dear familiar greeting, but lots of other cakes become more meaningful when you write a note on them. Wish many more happy years to an anniversary couple, congratulate the friend who's just had a business promotion or the student who's earned an "A". Wish "bon voyage" to travelers, welcome a new baby or say "so long" to departing neighbors.

The skill of writing or printing in icing is quickly learned. Even if your handwriting is less than perfect, with a little practice you'll be able to do clear, beautiful script and printing.

A great big beautiful birthday card

Here's a sheet cake where the birthday greeting is the decoration! While most messages are piped with round tubes, a star tube can produce a striking effect with large characters. A pattern makes it easy to do. When the cake is finished, light it up with candles and present it to the birthday child. She'll be overwhelmed—and so will all the rest of the guests.

1. Bake and chill two 9" x 13" layers. Fill, then ice smoothly with buttercream. Transfer greeting pattern (see Appendix, starting page 162) to cake top. Set cake on foil-covered board.

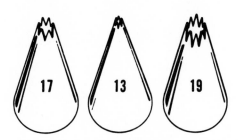

Star tubes make quick work of lettering and borders

2. Do the orange message first with tube 17. Hold the cone at a 45° angle and start with the little twirl that appears on most letters, then move into the plain line. The technique is similar to making a curved shell, page 33. When a stroke ends in a second twirl, as the "H" in "HAPPY", add this twirl after the stroke is completed, blending it in to the straight line. Add the pink stars with tube 17. Pipe the name within heart with tube 13.

3. Cover the sides of the cake with giant up-and-down zigzags piped with tube 19. Use the same tube to do the top shell border and rosette base border. This delicious birthday card serves 24.

Begin your practice with simple block letters

Use tube 2 or any small round tube for practice. Keep an even pressure as you glide over the surface

Printing in icing is really only piping a series of lines—horizontal, vertical, diagonal and curved. Three things are essential to learn to print clear attractive letters. *First*, make sure your icing is properly thinned. Practice with buttercream (page 22), thinned as recipe suggests. Try a few strokes to be sure the icing flows out easily—too thick and the fine lines will break. *Second*, you must use the correct hand position—as close to horizontal as possible. Review page 30 to see this position. *Third*, as with all skills, practice is necessary. Spend just five or ten minutes a day for a week—you'll be amazed at your progress.

Tape the pattern for block letters (Appendix, starting page 162) to the back of a cookie sheet and tape wax paper over. Fit a decorating cone with tube 2 and fill with thinned icing. Do a few lines first, straight and curved, breaking off cleanly. Rest your tube *very lightly* on the pan, letting it glide back and forth, just touching. After your hand has achieved an easy control, pipe a few messages freehand.

Pipe a message on a pretty cake

1

2

3

Show off your lettering talents by decorating this rosy cake. Begin by piping some tube 225 flowers with tube 2 centers in royal icing. Dry.

1. Bake, chill and fill two 10" round cake layers. Ice in buttercream and set on cake board. Pipe a tight zig-zag border with tube 17 at base.

To make it easier to space the message, prepare a paper pattern. Trace an 8" cake circle, then trace a 6" circle within it. Print 1" high letters within the lines, spacing carefully. Note that all vertical lines point to the center of the circle. Transfer to cake top by pricking through the pattern with a pin.

2. Pipe the letters with tube 3 and thinned icing, holding cone flat as possible and just gliding over the surface. Now pipe a spray of stems and attach short branches with the same tube and icing. The technique for the curved lines of the spray is exactly the same as for the letters. With pink thinned icing, drop a double row of tube 3 strings from top edge of cake.

3. Use tube 17 to pipe shallow curves on cake top, from point to point of string drapes. Add rosettes with same tube.

Now attach flowers to the spray by piping a dot of icing on the back of each. Trim the flowers with tube 65 leaves, piped with thinned icing. We finished off the pretty picture with a little graduate's cap. The cake serves 14.

Use the same design for any number of party cakes—varying the message to suit the occasion, and changing the color scheme as you wish. As you gain control, you'll be able to pipe the message freehand, without a pattern.

3   17   65

Practice script writing for control and ease

After you've had a little practice piping script, you'll be pleasantly surprised. Even if your handwriting is imperfect, you'll be able to pipe beautiful curved characters in icing! That's because you're using your whole arm from the shoulder, not just your fingers. Script writing is based on the same essentials as block printing: properly thinned icing, the correct hand position shown on page 30, and practice. Fill a decorating cone fitted with tube 2 with thinned icing and begin practice by tracing the script pattern in the Appendix, starting page 162. Tape pattern to cookie sheet and cover with wax paper.

Touching the tube lightly to the surface, and holding cone almost flat, first try a few curves as shown above. Now pipe some initials, making curves smooth and even, and just gliding over the surface. Add lower case letters to an initial to spell out a message. Practice a few minutes a day for a week—your writing will become easy and almost effortless.

Use tube 2 for practice. Be sure the icing is properly thinned so it flows out easily

Graceful script curves across a party cake

Script is the feature on this cake, and isn't it effective? Decorate it to show a special person just how much you appreciate him.

1. Bake, chill and fill a 10" round two-layer cake, then ice smoothly in buttercream. Divide side into tenths and mark about 1" below top edge.

2. Pipe a tube 6 ball border at base, then trim with tube 2 balls. With thinned icing, drop four rows of tube 2 string from mark to mark on cake side. Add a fleur-de-lis and three dots at points of string drapes.

3. Stir an equal amount of piping gel into icing for the script. To help you position it on the cake, practice on the back of a 10" cake pan first. Now glide tube 2, held almost flat, across the surface of the cake top, adding easy curves to the initials and final letters. Trim with little dots of icing.

Finish the cake with a triple tube 4 top border. (A similar one is shown on page 39.) Serves 14 guests.

Round tubes pipe all the trim

CHAPTER TWELVE

It's easy to weave a basket in icing

Yes, one or two tubes and your own skilled hands can pipe an amazingly realistic basket that looks just like one made of straw or reed. After just a little practice you'll be able to turn out this cake-top ornament.

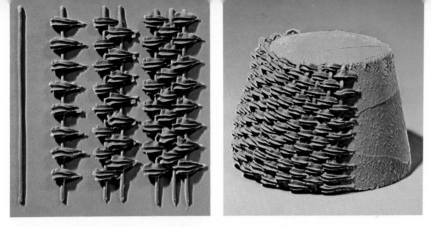

First practice the technique

You'll need two decorating cones, one fitted with tube 3, the other with tube 16. We suggest you use royal icing. Practice on the back of a pan propped upright securely, or on a practice board.

1. With tube 3, pipe a vertical line of icing about 4" long. Attach icing at top and let the string fall with tube held slightly above surface. Now use tube 16 to cross the line with small horizontal shells from top to bottom. Leave about ⅜" of space between them. Keep the tube you are not using covered with a damp towel.

2. Use tube 3 again to pipe a second vertical line, just at the tails of the shells. Now pipe tube 16 shells across this line just as before, positioning each between the shells crossing the first line.

3. Continue dropping vertical lines and crossing them with shells. See how the weave emerges! Practice long enough so your hand gets the feel of the technique and your vertical lines are evenly spaced.

Now weave the little basket

For this project we are using a styrofoam shape and royal icing to create a lasting little art object. Let it glorify a special cake, then save it for a pretty decorative accent.

1. Cut a 4" thick piece of styrofoam into a basket shape, 5" in diameter at top, tapering to about 4½" at base. Cookie cutters will help to mark the top and bottom—carve with any sharp knife. Ice the styrofoam and dry.

2. Place the basket on its 5" diameter side and weave the basket just as described above. Allow the tube 3 lines to fan out slightly to accommodate the tapered shape. Dry, then set the basket upright and pipe an arc of curved shells with tube 16 on opposite sides for handles. Finish the top edge with a curved shell border done with the same tube.

Pipe the brown-eyed susans

You'll need about three dozen for the bouquet. The technique is very similar to that of the daisy on page 97. Use royal icing for these lasting blooms. First pipe the flower centers.

1. Holding your decorating cone straight up, pipe tube 6 brown cone-shaped mounds on wax paper. Sprinkle with brown-tinted sugar and allow to dry.

2. Now pull out slender petals with tube 103 on your flower nail, just as you do for a daisy. Immediately incise two lines on each petal with a damp artist's brush. Slide the flower into a curved surface and press a brown cone into the center. Dry thoroughly.

Pipe leaves on wire stems with tube 67 as shown on page 104. The same page shows how to mount the flowers on 6" stems.

3. Heap green royal icing on the basket surface and pull it up with your spatula for a grassy effect. Clip the stems of the flowers and leaves to various lengths, and insert them into the basket, starting with the center flowers with the longest stems. Let this blossoming little creation dry, and display it with pride! If you plan to put it on a cake, first center a 5" circle of plastic wrap on the cake top, then set the basket on it.

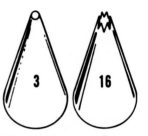

Many tubes can be used for basket weaving. For this one, we are using a plain round tube and a star tube.

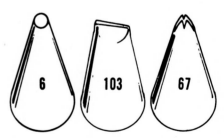

The brown-eyed susan is first cousin to the daisy. Centers are piped separately.

141

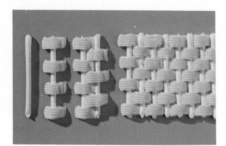

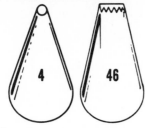

Combine tubes 4 and 46 for basket-weaving with a different look.

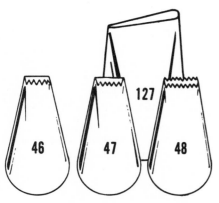

Tubes 46, 47 and 48 are called basket-weaving tubes. Tube 127 pipes a big rose

Baskets of flowers are decorators' favorites

Some of the prettiest cakes are replicas of flower-filled baskets. They never fail to bring forth exclamations of delight, and they're really quite easy to do. Practice a different style of basket weaving and see the effect of contrasting colors. Fit one decorating cone with tube 4 and fill with white icing. Fit a second cone with tube 46 and fill with yellow icing.

On a practice board, or propped-up cookie sheet, drop a line with tube 4. Holding tube perpendicular to surface, touch and apply pressure to attach. Lift slightly and drop straight down. Touch again, release pressure and draw away.

With tube 46, cross the line with short bands of icing, leaving spaces between them about the same width as the bands. Continue dropping strings and crossing them until you have woven a 4″ or 5″ section.

Fill a basket with roses

Big full-blown roses fill a pretty yellow and white basket. Large tubes are used so you can decorate this centerpiece cake in a hurry.

1. Make the buttercream roses first with tube 127, following directions on page 101. You'll need about 18. Air-dry the flowers if the weather is dry, if not, freeze them.

2. Bake a two-layer cake in 8″ or 9″ pans. If the top of the top layer is rounded, don't trim it off level—it will serve as a background for the roses. Fill the layers and ice the cake smoothly in white buttercream. Place it on a cake board, and if you like, add a fluffy cake ruffle, pushing the sewn end under the cake with a small knife.

3. Now weave the basket. This time use tube 48 for the vertical lines, tube 46 for the horizontal bands. Follow the directions given above. Pipe the puffy rope border at base with tube 4-B curved shells, then finish the top with stars piped with the same tube.

Arrange the roses on top, piping a mound of icing on the back of each to secure. Add a few tube 67 leaves. This pretty basket serves ten.

Tube 13 weaves the baskets, fills them with flowers and ties them with bows

Decorate this sweet surprise in just a short time and present it with pride to the birthday child! The petal shape of the cake gives you a perfect background for the baskets with no measuring needed—just one tube does all the trim.

1. Bake a two-layer cake in 9″ petal-shaped pans. Fill the layers and ice smoothly as directed in Chapter Two. Transfer basket pattern to each curve of the cake side. (See Appendix, starting on page 162.)

2. Use tube 13 for all decorating. First weave the baskets, just as directed on page 141. Space the vertical lines slightly farther apart at the top of the basket and taper in toward the base. Pipe the handles in a rope design with curved shells set close together.

3. Fill each basket with five star flowers. Pipe six shell petals for each flower. When all are piped, add yellow stars for centers. At base of cake, fill in between baskets with shells and add a shell border at top of cake. Pipe green curves of icing around basket handles and over top border. Make figure eight bows and add streamers. Insert candles in holders and light up your sparkling creation! Serves eight, very generously, or sixteen dainty slices.

CHAPTER THIRTEEN

Tier cakes...
the decorator's
crowning achievement

For every decorator, the first tier cake is a joy—and a challenge sometimes faced with a little timidity. But take courage! A tier cake is really just a group of smaller cakes, now called tiers, each decorated with techniques you already know well.

Review the information on pages 24 and 25 on preparing and icing the tiers. Since a tier cake is most often a wedding cake, and is the center of all eyes at the bridal reception, you will want to be sure that each tier is smoothly covered with icing to be a perfect background for all the lovely trims. Buttercream is used most often.

Well before you begin, decide on the number of servings needed. Page 162 lists the customary servings each tier will provide—but follow the customs in your own community. Then plan your cake accordingly. Most brides freeze the top tier for the first anniversary, so the servings for that tier are listed separately.

And most important—follow the directions for building your many-tiered creation that are explained on pages 146 and 147.

Sweet Dreams . . . a dainty, ruffled bridal cake

Tiny drop flowers and polka dots give a pretty "printed" effect to the tiers, finished off with feminine ruffles. This is a charming cake for an intimate reception, and one very easy to decorate.

1. Make trims in advance. First pipe many royal icing drop flowers with tube 225, add tube 2 centers and dry. Pipe about 24 larger flowers with tubes 2E and 1G and center each with tube 13. After drying, mount flowers on wire stems as shown on page 104. Pipe tube 67 leaves on wire stems. When dry, twist the stems together to form a little bouquet.

2. Bake the tiers, a two-layer 12" round tier, each layer about 2" high, and a two-layer 8" round tier, each layer about 1½" high. Fill and ice each smoothly with buttercream.

Cover a double-thick 16" cake board with foil. Assemble tiers on cake board as shown on the top of the next page.

3. Decorate base tier. Divide tier side into twelfths and mark on top edge. (See page 42.) Make a second series of marks about 1" above base, each mark midway between marks on top edge. Pipe a tube 8 bottom ball border. Drop a tube 3 string guideline from mark to mark above border, then pipe a tube 104 ruffle over guideline, holding wide end of tube against tier side and narrow end almost straight out. Finish the ruffle with tube 3 beading. Drop guidelines and pipe ruffles from top edge of tier the same way. Pipe a tube 6 top ball border.

4. Divide 8" tier into eighths, and mark about 1" down from top edge. Pipe a tube 6 ball border at base. Drop tube 3 guidelines from mark to mark, then pipe ruffles and beading. Add a tube 6 top ball border.

5. Finish the cake by attaching the small flowers with dots of icing as shown in the picture. Complete the design by piping tube 1 polka dots between the flowers. Insert a Flower Spike in center of top tier and set your little bouquet in it. Base tier serves 68 guests, the top tier serves 30.

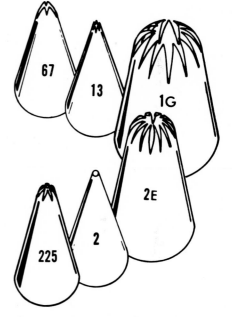

Quick-to-pipe drop flowers pattern the cake

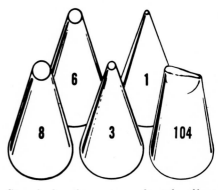

Simple borders give a lavish effect

How to put a tier cake together

It is most important to construct your architectural masterpiece strongly and safely. The weight of each tier rests on the one below it, and the combined weight of all upper tiers rest on the base tier. Therefore a system of dowel supports must be utilized to assure a beautiful cake whose tiers will never shift or lean. Tier cakes may be stacked, one tier on another, or separated by pillars and separator plates.

The dowel method of constructing a cake with stacked tiers

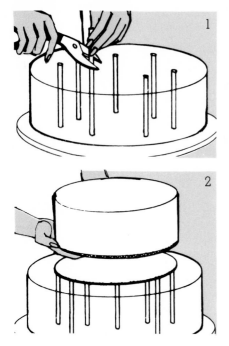

This procedure should be used for any stacked cake or on a stacked portion of a cake, such as the one on page 150. The principle is to insert dowels for support in any tier with one or more above it. Only the top tier needs no support. Here we use the cake on page 144 as an example.

1. Set the iced base tier on a strong cake board or tray. Attach securely by stroking the board with royal icing or corn syrup. Use a cardboard cake circle one size smaller than the tier above to lightly mark a circle on top of tier—in this case a 6" circle since the upper tier is 8" in diameter. Within this marked circle, insert seven ¼" dowel rods. Push each dowel down to cake base, then lift up and clip off exposed portion with a pruning shears or wire cutter. Push down again. (Use seven dowels where diameter of tier above is 10" or less. The larger and more numerous the tiers above, the more dowels needed.)

2. Wrap a cake circle the same size as second tier with clear plastic, and center it on the base tier. The plastic will make it easy to disassemble the cake for serving. Place the second tier, already iced, in position, attaching it with a few strokes of royal icing or syrup.

To prevent the tiers from slipping sideways, sharpen a long ¼" dowel rod and push it through both tiers, down to the cake board. Lift up to clip off exposed portion, then push down again, level with the cake top. The cake it now ready to decorate. Follow the same procedure for any stacked tier cake, regardless of the number of tiers.

The dowel method of constructing a cake with pillars

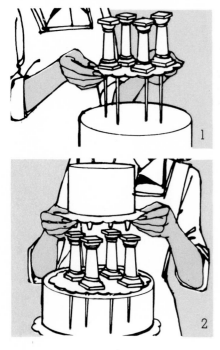

Pillars give a tier cake an extra lift and make them even more dramatic. Pillars come in many styles to complement the design of your cake and are always used with plastic separator plates. Purchase them in sets, or buy pillars and plates separately to make your own set. Use plates 1" or 2" larger in diameter than the tier which rests upon them. This allows ample space for any borders or side trim. Here we are using the cake shown on page 157 as an example.

1. Set the 16" base tier on a sturdy cake board or serving tray, securing it with a few strokes of royal icing or corn syrup. Gently press a 10" cake circle on the tier top to mark a circle. Within this circle, insert eleven ¼" dowel rods and clip off level with top of tier, just as described above for a stacked cake. Set the four pillars in position on a 14" separator plate, then snap the pegs supplied with the plate to the underside of the plate. Gently push the plate into the tier until the plate rests on top of tier.

Now set the middle 12" iced tier on a second 14" plate, securing with royal icing or corn syrup. Set the plate on the pillars rising from the base tier. Attach pillars and pegs to a 10" separator plate and push the plate into the tier, just as you did for the base tier.

2. Place top 8" tier, already iced, on a second 10" plate, securing with icing or corn syrup. Set on pillars rising from middle tier. Now decorate the assembled cake.

Use this method of construction for any pillared tier cake.

A second method uses clear dividers instead of pillars

This is an easy method of tier cake construction and gives the finished cake an airy, floating appearance. The divider set consists of plastic plates ranging in size from 6" to 16" and clear plastic legs, 7½" tall, that are pushed right through the cake tier.

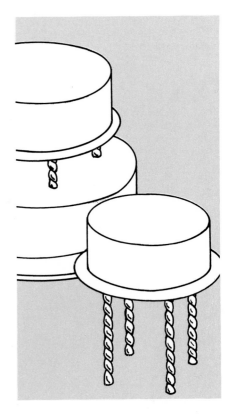

1. Let's use the cake on page 155 as an example. Set the iced base 14" tier on a sturdy 18" cake board or serving tray, securing with strokes of royal icing or corn syrup. Center the iced middle 10" tier on a 12" separator plate, again securing with royal icing or syrup. Fit legs into the four receptacles on the underside of the plate. Hold the tier by the edge of the plate above the base tier, let legs rest on the tier surface, then gently press until legs touch cake base below 14" tier.

2. Secure 6" tier on an 8" separator plate, insert legs and center above middle tier. Push legs through tier to touch cake base. The cake is now assembled and ready to decorate.

You may remove plates and tiers from tops of legs and decorate each tier individually, then reassemble. Do most of the decorating while the cake is assembled to insure that all side trims line up evenly.

Some tips for successful tier cakes

The cake board for a tier cake is important to its appearance and for ease in transporting. Of course, a silver or crystal tray is ideal, but if you do not have one large enough, a cake board is a good substitute. Use two or three thicknesses of corrugated cardboard, taped together with the grain running in opposite directions. Remember, a tier cake is heavy! Make sure the board is at least 2" larger all around than the base tier. Cover it smoothly with foil in a color that complements the cake trim. You may want to dress up the board with doilies or a cake ruffle.

Use the bridal couple's favorite flavor for cake and filling. While a white cake is traditional, almost any mix or recipe is suitable. Use their favorite filling, too—just avoid a custard or other mixture that spoils quickly. Buttercream is the usual choice for icing and borders.

Keep tiers in proportion. After you've looked through this chapter you might decide to design your own wedding creation, following your own ideas and the bride's wishes. A good all-around rule for tier sizes is to make each upper tier 4" smaller than the one below. it. Thus you might have 16", 12" and 8" tiers. For fewer servings, the tiers would be 14", 10" and 6". Lower tiers are usually about 4" high, the top tier 3" high.

Plan ahead. This is important for any decorated cake, but essential for a lavish tier cake. Bake the tiers even weeks ahead and freeze them. Royal icing flowers and other trims can be done weeks in advance, too. Decide on the top and between-tiers ornaments so they are at hand when you need them. You may ice and assemble the tiers the day before decorating—the icing will keep the cake moist. With this advance planning, the decorating itself is a joy, not a chore. Start with the base tier and work your way up to the top.

How to carry a tier cake

Once you've completed your towering creation, you'll want to be sure it arrives at the reception in perfect condition. Here's the way to do it. If the tiers are on pillars, lift off each one, on its plate. Carve a ½" depression, the exact shape and size of the separator plate or cake board in a 3" thick piece of soft foam. Set the tiers in the depressions, then on a level surface. The back of a station wagon is ideal, but if you are carrying the cake in a car, first build a level platform to cover the back seat. Drape light plastic cleaner's bags over the tiers to protect them from dust and sun. Reassemble the cake at the reception. Transport a stacked cake the same way, but without disassembling the tiers.

Even a little cake looks impressive when the tiers are given a lift

One cake mix or recipe, three miniature pans and a little tier separator set, just like one for a large wedding cake, makes a tiny tier cake with a lot of drama! These three charmers show how you can decorate the tiers to suit the seasons. We've added candles to turn them into memorable birthday centerpieces. Each cake serves twelve. Top tier cuts into two servings, middle tier four and base tier makes six servings.

Each cake starts the same. Bake the one-layer round tiers in 5", 6½" and 8" pans. Ice each tier then attach two upper tiers to 5½" and 7" separator plates with a few strokes of icing. Snap in the clear plastic legs. Set 8" tier on a cake board or serving tray, then assemble the tiers just as described on page 147. Now let your imagination take over and decorate your miniature masterpiece.

All cakes take one recipe or mix, all serve twelve guests

Violets garland a spring birthday cake

1. Make royal icing violets in advance in varied shades of lavender. See directions, page 97, and use tubes 101 and 1. Bake, ice and assemble the tiers as described above.

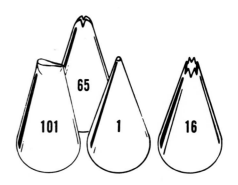

2. Tube 16 pipes all the borders. Pipe a garland border at base of all tiers and pipe a star between each garland. Frame the garlands on base tier with a tight zigzag. Now pipe a top shell border on all three tiers. Pipe a heavy curving line of icing across top of base tier, extending down side, and attach flowers with dots of icing. Trim the two upper tiers the same way. Add leaves with tube 65. Crown with a single candle. We added a quartet of bluebirds to enhance the spring theme.

A star crowns winter's snow-white cake

1. Make the snowflakes in advance, using royal icing and the patterns in the Appendix, starting page 162. The method is described on page 59.

Pipe and over-pipe all stars with royal icing and tube 2. You will need two stars for tops of two lower tiers, one whole and two half-stars for top ornament—all dried flat. Sprinkle with edible glitter as soon as they are piped. For snowflakes on sides of tiers, tape patterns to curved sides of pans, prop with crumpled foil, then tape wax paper over and pipe.

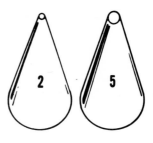

To assemble top ornament, pipe a line of royal icing down center of whole star. Lay a 5" length of stiff florists' wire on it, pipe a second line of icing on wire and set a half-star on it. Prop with cotton balls to dry. Carefully turn over, prop again, pipe a line of icing on center of other side of whole star. Set second half-star on it, prop again to dry.

2. Bake and ice the tiers. Attach flat stars to tops of two lower tiers with icing. Assemble tiers and pipe tube 5 ball borders on all edges. Secure curved stars to tier sides with icing, then push in top star ornament. Insert push-in candle holders and candles around side of top tier.

Brilliant leaves drift across an autumn cake

1. Make the maple leaves ahead in marzipan. Use the recipe on page 85, tint portions in warm autumn hues and roll out thin on a surface well dusted with confectioners' sugar, just like pie dough. Cut the leaves with leaf-shaped cutters, dry within a curved surface. For realism, you can paint veins with thinned food color and add florists' wire stems with a little royal icing.

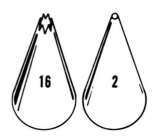

2. Bake, ice and assemble the cake. Borders are done mainly with tube 16. Pipe a rosette border at bottom of base tier, a star border at top. On middle tier, pipe a rosette border at bottom. Divide side into eighths, drop guidelines and pipe a zigzag curved garland. Drape with tube 2 strings and add a star border at top. Decorate top tier the same as middle tier. Insert push-in holders and candles around middle tier and add a single candle in top tier. Arrange leaves as picture shows, attaching with dots of icing.

149

Daisies trim a delightful summer wedding cake . . . cherubs dance on the tiers

Sunny pastel yellow icing sets off the bright-eyed daisies—the cherub ornament and pillars add a note of youthful gaiety. This cake is an example of how careful choice of pillars and ornament can make a simple cake outstanding.

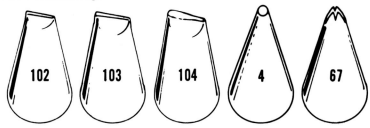

Pipe fresh-looking daisies in three sizes

Make flower trims in advance

Pipe royal icing daisies in three sizes, using tubes 102, 103 and 104. Pipe centers with tube 4, flatten with a fingertip and sprinkle with yellow-tinted granulated sugar. Dry flowers within curved surface. (See directions on pages 97 and 104.)

Attach wire stems to about two dozen daisies and pipe leaves on wire with tube 67. Fill a small decorative plastic bowl with a styrofoam half-ball, securing with royal icing. Twist stems of flowers and leaves together and arrange in bowl.

Bake and assemble the tiers

Bake and chill the two-layer square tiers—14", 10" and 6". Layers for two lower tiers should be about 2" high, layers for top tier about 1½" high. Fill and ice all tiers smoothly with buttercream.

This cake requires both pillared and stacked methods of assembly with dowels as described on page 146. Two 11" square separator plates and cupid pillars are used. Set 14" tier on an 18" square foil-covered cake board. Lightly press an 11" square separator plate to surface, remove and insert twelve ¼" dowel rods within marked square. Place separator plate on tier surface and attach pillars. Assemble the two upper tiers on the second 11" separator plate, using dowels for support in 10" tier. Set on pillars rising from base tier.

Decorate the assembled cake

1. Mark a curve with a toothpick on all sides of the base tier, starting about 2" in from the top corners. Do the same on the middle tier, starting about 1½" in from the corners. Mark curve on top tier from corner to corner. These will serve as guides for the flower garlands.

2. Edge all tiers with simple borders. Pipe a tube 4-B base star border on two lower tiers, lifting tube as the form builds up for a puffy effect. Pipe tube 32 base star border on top tier. Pipe top shell borders on all three tiers with tube 32.

3. Attach flowers to all tier sides with dots of icing, using marks as guides. Set bowl of flowers within pillars and trim base with flowers. Set dancing cupid ornament on top tier and ring all cupids with daisies. Finally, trim all flowers with tube 67 leaves.

The two lower tiers of this entrancing centerpiece will serve 148 wedding guests, the top tier will serve an additional 18 guests.

This is an easy cake to vary according to your own taste and that of the bride. White or blush pink roses against pink icing will give a romantic effect. Drop flowers in rainbow pastels against white icing will result in a cake with completely different personality.

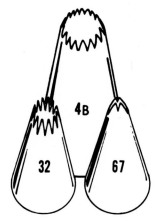

Simple borders edge the cake

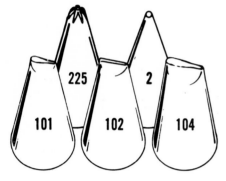

Sweetheart . . . an exquisite bridal cake
sentimental as a valentine

A wedding is a time for sentiment and Sweetheart displays many of the signs of love—heart-shaped pink tiers, ribbon-tied nosegays and cascades of roses and posies. And as a surprise—a miniature replica of the bridal cake for the bride to freeze for the first anniversary.

Make trims in advance

1. Pipe many royal icing roses and buds in three sizes using tubes 101, 102 and 104. The tubes 101 and 102 flowers will be used for the anniversary cake—flowers piped with tubes 102 and 104 will adorn the bridal cake. Pipe many tube 225 drop flowers with tube 2 centers. When flowers are dry, mount some of each size on wire stems and twist stems together into two nosegays, a little one for the anniversary cake, a larger one for the bridal cake. Tie with pink ribbon. Pipe royal icing spikes on the backs of a few larger roses (page 104).

2. Prepare the cake boards. Trace a 12" heart pan on paper, add 2" all around and use as a pattern to cut cake board for the bridal cake. Trace the 9" pan from the Heart Mini-tier set and add 1" all around for a pattern for the board for the small cake. Cover both with foil.

Prepare the cake tiers

1. Bake two-layer tiers for the bridal cake in 6", 9" and 12" heart tier pans. Layers for the 6" tier should be about 1½" high, for the two larger tiers about 2" high. Fill, ice and assemble on the large cake board, using 6" and 9" heart separator plates and six clear plastic legs. Follow the method described on page 147.

2. Bake single-layer tiers in Heart Mini-tier pans, 5", 7½" and 9". Ice and assemble with mini-heart separator plates and legs, just as you did for the larger cake.

With a small knife, push the sewn end of a cake ruffle beneath the base tier of both cakes.

Decorate the wedding cake

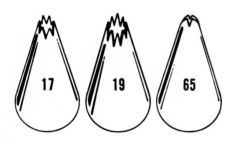

1. Divide each curving side of the three heart tiers into fifths and mark about 1½" up from base on two larger tiers, 1" up on top tier. Drop string guidelines for curved side trim. Cover all guidelines with curved shells piped with tube 17. Starting with bottom tier, pipe tube 19 shell borders at base of all tiers. Use tube 17 to pipe scalloped top borders.

2. Pipe a heavy curve of icing on two lower tiers and arrange flowers, attaching with dots of icing. Use spiked flowers on tier sides. Set a little bridal couple ornament on top of cake, then trim all flowers with tube 65 leaves. Lay the nosegay next to the ornament. The bride may give it to her maid of honor. The two lower tiers of Sweetheart serve 76 guests, top tier serves twelve wedding guests.

Decorate the anniversary cake

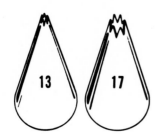

This is done in the same way as the wedding cake, but with smaller tubes. Divide each side of heart tiers into fifths, then pipe side trims with tube 13, base shell borders with tube 17 and top scallop borders with tube 13. Arrange flowers in curves, using smaller roses and buds. Set small nosegay on cake top. This petite anniversary cake will slice into twelve party-size pieces.

Delicate blue blossoms wreath a wedding cake

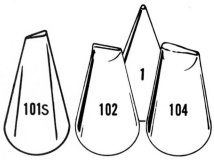

Pipe the flowers in advance

Here's the prettiest way to provide "something blue" for the bride! Dainty blue wild roses form heart shapes and garlands, even adorn the top ornament. Clear columns give an ethereal look.

Make trims and patterns in advance

1. First pipe the wild roses in royal icing. Use tubes 101s, 102 and 104 for varied sizes and add tube 1 centers. Dry and set aside.

2. Cut patterns for the tiers. First consult page 45. For the top of the base tier, fold a 14" paper circle in eighths, then cut a pointed arch near the curved edge of the paper. To check the pattern, insert the clear legs into a 12" separator plate and set on the unfolded pattern. There should be space for each leg within the arches. Correct pattern if necessary.

Cut patterns for the two upper tier tops the same way, using 10" and 6" paper circles. Check pattern for middle tier by placing an 8" plate, legs attached, on it. Cut 3" x 3" heart pattern for base tier by folding a piece of paper in half, sketching a half-heart, then cutting out.

Prepare the cake tiers

1. Bake three tiers—a two-layer 14" tier, each layer 2" high, a two-layer 10" tier, each layer 2" high, and a two-layer 6" tier, each layer 1½" high. Fill and ice each tier smoothly in buttercream. Place 14" tier on an 18" round cake board, 10" tier on a 12" separator plate and 6" tier on an 8" separator plate. Trace patterns with a toothpick on all three tier tops. Attach clear legs to the plates and assemble the tiers, just as explained on page 147. Make sure top patterns line up, one with another.

2. Mark position of hearts, flower garlands and string drapes on tiers with a toothpick. This is easy to do without measuring by using clear legs as guides. On base tier, mark top edge directly out from each leg, then mark halfway between each mark. Make a second series of marks on cake side, 1½" up from base of tier and directly below original marks. Trace heart pattern eight times on tier side and top, positioning lower points of hearts on marks on tier side. On middle tier, divide side into eighths, again using legs as guides, and mark about 1" down from top edge. Divide top tier into eighths at top edge, using legs as guides.

Decorate the cake

1. Pipe a shell border at bottom and top of base tier with tube 32. Remove upper two tiers on plates to make it easier to pipe the tier top trim. Outline the marked pattern with tight zigzags with tube 13, then top with tube 2 beading. Attach flowers to tier side with dots of icing, following marked heart pattern. Use larger flowers here.

2. On middle tier, pipe a tube 32 shell border at base, then edge with tube 13 shells. Pipe a tube 19 shell border at top of tier. Pipe top design with tubes 13 and 2, just as for base tier. Drop string guidelines for flower garlands with tube 2. Top guidelines with double bows piped with same tube. Attach medium and small flowers on dots of icing.

3. Pipe a tube 19 shell border at base of top tier, then circle with tube 13 shells. Pipe top design with tubes 13 and 2, just as for two other tiers. Drop triple strings from mark to mark on top edge of cake. Pipe a tube 16 top shell border. Pipe four tube 2 bows on cake side, and add a cluster of the smallest flowers below them, securing with dots of icing. Pipe four tube 2 hearts between flower clusters.

4. Add the final touches. Attach flowers to bases of all legs. On base tier, attach pairs of tiny plastic doves between legs with icing. Place a little cupid figure on middle tier and trim with flowers. Trim top ornament with flowers, attaching with royal icing. Trim all flowers with tube 65 leaves. Two lower tiers of this delicate bridal confection serve 140 guests, top tier serves 16.

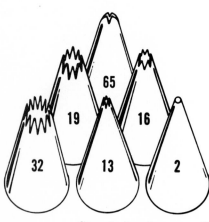

Simple borders set off the flower trim

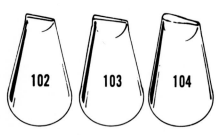

*Pipe roses and buds in
varied sizes and tints*

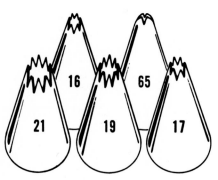

*Simple borders are
background for the flowers*

Love's Flower . . . a blushing masterpiece

garlanded with pink roses

For many centuries roses have been known as beloved symbols of love and romance. Poets have made them the subject of their songs. Artists have painted them and artisans worked them into jewelled ornaments and tapestries. Here the beautiful rose is the lavish trim of the center-piece cake, especially appropriate for a June bride, lovely for a wedding at any season.

Pipe roses in profusion

Well ahead of time, pipe the royal icing roses and buds. Use several tints of pink for a subtle effect. Follow the directions on pages 96 and 101 and use tubes 102, 103 and 104 for varied sizes. Set aside to dry, then pipe spikes on the backs of most of the flowers (see page 104). Store carefully until decorating day.

Prepare the cake tiers

1. *Love's Flower* is a big cake for a large reception. Bake and fill three round tiers, each two layers—16", 12" and 8". Layers for the two larger tiers should be 2" high, for the top 8" tier, 1½" high.

2. Ice the tiers smoothly with buttercream in the palest tint of pink. This color will be used for all borders too. Assemble on a large tray or 20" sturdy cake board, following method on page 146. Use 14" separator plates and 5" pillars between two lower tiers. Use 10" separator plates and 3" pillars between middle tier and top tier.

Decorate the wedding cake

1. Simple borders set off the roses. Divide base tier into eighths, and mark at top edge, using pillars as guides. Pipe bottom shell border with tube 21. Drop a string guideline from mark to mark at top of tier. This will serve to define the flower garlands. Pipe top shell border with tube 19 and edge separator plate with scallops, using same tube.

2. On middle tier, pipe base shell border with tube 19. Divide and mark top edge in eighths, using pillars as guides. Drop string guidelines for flower garlands. Pipe tube 17 top shell border and scallops around separator plate.

3. On top tier, use the method on page 42 to divide and mark top edge in eighths. Drop string guidelines for garlands from mark to mark. Pipe a tube 17 base shell border. Use tube 16 to pipe "e" motion garlands over guidelines, and add a tube 16 top shell border.

Finish with roses and ornaments

1. For base tier, trim a double wedding ring ornament with a rose, securing with royal icing. Remove ornament base first. Set within pillars. Arrange roses and buds in curves on separator plate. Following guidelines, attach spiked flowers to tier side in garlands, first piping a mound of icing on spikes.

2. For middle tier, arrange a cluster of roses and buds on separator plate, using royal icing as glue. Attach spiked flowers in garlands on tier side, just as for base tier.

3. For top tier, trim a second double ring ornament with a rose. Set on tier top and add rosebuds at base. Attach a spiked rose within each garland on tier side.

Trim all flowers with tube 65 leaves. *Love's Flower* is ready to take its place on the reception table. The two lower tiers serve 186 wedding guests, the top tier 30.

Wedding Waltz . . . an exquisite bridal creation

Graceful curving borders and fresh flowers combine to make an outstanding cake—simple and very elegant.

Wedding Waltz is pure white, the only touch of color is the little blue ribbon in the flowers that crown the tiers—but if you prefer, match pastel flowers to those in the bride's bouquet.

Prepare the cake tiers

A somewhat unusual proportion is used for *Wedding Waltz*. Bake and fill three round, two-layer tiers—16", 10" and 6". Make the layers for the 6" tier 1½" high, for the two larger tiers 2" high.

Ice the tiers smoothly with buttercream, then assemble on a 20" foil-covered cake board. Use the stacked dowel method described on page 146, but set the 10" tier slightly to the rear of the 16" tier to allow room for flowers and the cupid ornament.

Unusual borders are piped with star tubes and trimmed with string

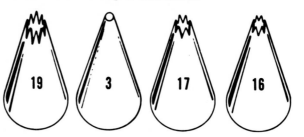

Decorate the wedding cake

1. On base tier, divide and mark top edge into twelfths. Pipe a tube 19 bottom shell border. Leave two of the marked spaces on top edge of tier open. Make a second series of marks 1½" away from original marks.

In each of these spaces, pipe double tube 19 shells, curving over edge of tier. Now drop single and triple tube 3 strings, first below shells, then between them. ½" in from top edge pipe a tube 16 shell border. Within border pipe tube 3 scallops.

2. Divide middle tier into sixths and mark at top edge. Using marks as guides, gently press a plastic pattern press into tier side—or transfer pattern from Appendix, starting page 162. Pipe a tube 17 bottom shell border. Do side designs with tube 16 and curved shells. Pipe a tube 19 upright shell between each design. Do tube 16 top shell border.

3. On top tier, pipe a tube 16 base shell border. Divide side into sixths and mark at top edge. Pipe double shells at each mark, tops curving over edge. Drop double strings from shells and add little twirls with tube 3. ½" in from edge, pipe a tube 16 shell border on top of cake.

Finish the cake with flowers

1. Pack Oasis (obtainable at florists) into a small decorative vase. Insert stems of fresh flowers to form a bouquet. Add a ribbon bow and set vase on top of cake.

2. Set cupid ornament on center of base tier, attaching with mounds of icing. Insert a Flower Spike on an angle on side of tier just below cupid, one in top of tier just beside him, and one in side of middle tier. Fill spikes with water, using an eye-dropper. Arrange flowers in spikes.

Center elegant *Wedding Waltz* on the reception table. It will delight the bride and win the admiration of all the guests. The two lower tiers serve 166, the top tier serves 16 wedding guests.

**Just Wonderful . . .
every young bride's
dream of a wedding cake**

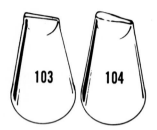

*Pipe sweet peas in two sizes,
two pretty pastels*

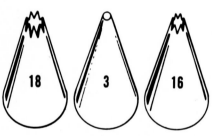

*Simple star tube borders
are dressed up with string*

1. Make trims in advance. Pipe the flowers. Use tubes 103 and 104 and the method on page 96 to pipe the royal icing sweet peas. You'll need a great many, but these flowers are the quickest and easiest to pipe. We chose tints of pale pink and delicate peach. Set aside to dry.

2. Sugar mold the hearts, using method on page 105 and 1" heart candy molds. You'll need about 35, but make a few extras. As soon as the shapes are unmolded, sprinkle with edible glitter.

3. Make the ornaments. For the between-tiers ornament, ice a styrofoam half-ball, about 4" in diameter. Dry. Starting at the bottom, cover the ball with sweet peas, attaching each with a dot of royal icing.

For the top ornament, add stems to sugar hearts. You'll need a dozen stemmed hearts. Pipe a little mound of royal icing on the flat side of a heart, lay a 6" length of florists' wire on it, and press on a second heart. Lay on tray to dry, then cover seams with tube 2 royal icing beading. Dry again, then tie a little ribbon bow to each wire stem. Twist stems together to form a bouquet and push into a block of styrofoam until needed. Tie eight bows for pillar trim.

Prepare and decorate the tiers

1. Bake and fill three round tiers—a two-layer 14", each layer 2" high—a two-layer 10", each layer 2" high—and a two-layer 6", each layer 1½" high. Ice smoothly, then assemble on an 18" cake board as shown on page 146. Use 12" separator plates and 7½" pillars between two lower tiers. Use 8" separator plates and 7½" pillars between middle and top tiers.

2. Divide base tier into twelfths, using pillars as guides, and mark on top edge of tier. Mark again about 1½" up from bottom of tier. Pipe a tube 18 shell border at base. Drop tube 3 string guidelines from marks above border. This will be used to define flower garlands. Starting and stopping ½" away from marks at top of tier, drop string guidelines, then pipe tube 18 zigzag garlands. Drop triple tube 3 strings over garlands, then add a tube 16 top shell border. Outline the edge of the separator plate with scallops piped with same tube.

3. On middle tier, divide side into twelfths and mark about 1½" above bottom of tier. Pipe a tube 18 base shell border, then drop tube 3 string guidelines from mark to mark. Pipe tube 18 zigzag garlands over guidelines, then drop triple tube 3 strings, adding a little twirl at points. Pipe a tube 16 reverse shell border at top of tier, and edge separator plate with tube 16 scallops.

4. Divide side of top tier into sixths and mark at top edge. Pipe a tube 18 base shell border. Drop string guidelines from mark to mark to define flower garlands. Pipe a tube 16 reverse shell top border.

Add flowers and ornaments

1. On bottom tier, make flower garlands following guidelines, attaching each flower with a dot of icing. Pipe mounds of icing on backs of hearts and press to side of tier above garlands. Set flower half-ball within pillars, attaching with a few strokes of royal icing. Review page 96, and make twelve small cascades of sweet peas around top edge of tier. Secure a ribbon bow with royal icing to base of each pillar.

2. On middle tier, make four cascades of flowers leading out from pillars. Set a plastic cupid within pillars and ring with flowers. Secure hearts to tier side and add bows to base of pillars.

3. Push a Flower Spike in center of top tier and insert heart bouquet. Surround with sweet peas. Use more flowers to form the garlands.

Just Wonderful is finished. Two lower tiers serve 140, top tier serves 16.

Cake serving and cutting guides and the patterns you need for cakes in this book

On this page are diagrams and charts to show you just how a tiered wedding cake is cut, and the servings each tier provides. The customary size of a wedding cake serving is a slice 1″ wide, 2″ deep and two layers high. Grooms' cakes are cut in the same size servings. See an actual size photograph of such a serving on page 27. If customs in your community require larger servings, 2″ wide, the number of servings will be half those listed here. Remember, most brides save the top tier to freeze for the first anniversary celebration.

To cut any tier cake, first lift off the top tier, then remove the second tier and cut it. Work your way down and cut the base tier last.

Wedding cake serving chart

This chart shows you the approximate number of two-layer servings each tier provides.

TIER SHAPE	SIZE	SERVINGS
ROUND	6″	16
	8″	30
	10″	48
	12″	68
	14″	92
	16″	118
	18″	148
SQUARE	6″	18
	8″	32
	10″	50
	12″	72
	14″	98
	16″	128
	18″	162
HEXAGON	6″	6
	9″	22
	12″	50
	15″	66
PETAL	6″	8
	9″	20
	12″	44
	15″	62
HEART	6″	12
	9″	28
	12″	48
	15″	90
RECTANGLE	9″x13″	54
	11″x15″	77
	12″x18″	108

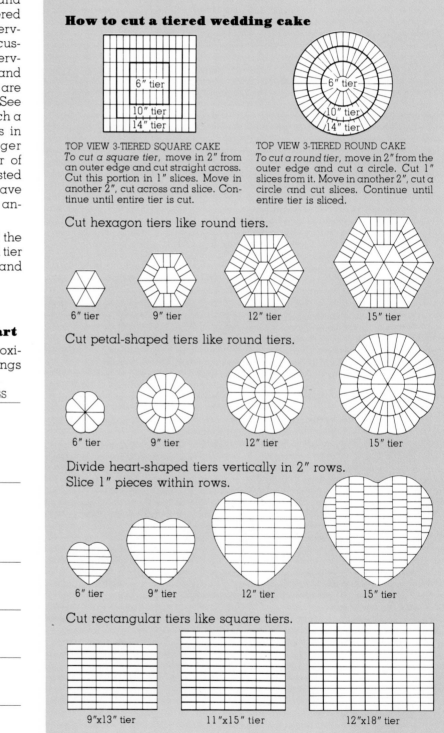

How to cut a tiered wedding cake

TOP VIEW 3-TIERED SQUARE CAKE
To cut a square tier, move in 2″ from an outer edge and cut straight across. Cut this portion in 1″ slices. Move in another 2″, cut across and slice. Continue until entire tier is cut.

TOP VIEW 3-TIERED ROUND CAKE
To cut a round tier, move in 2″ from the outer edge and cut a circle. Cut 1″ slices from it. Move in another 2″, cut a circle and cut slices. Continue until entire tier is sliced.

Cut hexagon tiers like round tiers.

Cut petal-shaped tiers like round tiers.

Divide heart-shaped tiers vertically in 2″ rows. Slice 1″ pieces within rows.

Cut rectangular tiers like square tiers.

Birthday cakes, shower cakes, or any cake not a bridal cake, are cut into larger dessert-size servings. This chart shows the method of cutting and the servings to be **expected** from various-sized cakes. Remember, the charts and servings listed below are for *two-layer* cakes.

To cut an unusually-shaped cake like the panda on page 15, cut the cake in half vertically. Lay cut sides down and slice. One-mix cakes of any shape serve twelve.

How to cut party cakes and number of servings each provides

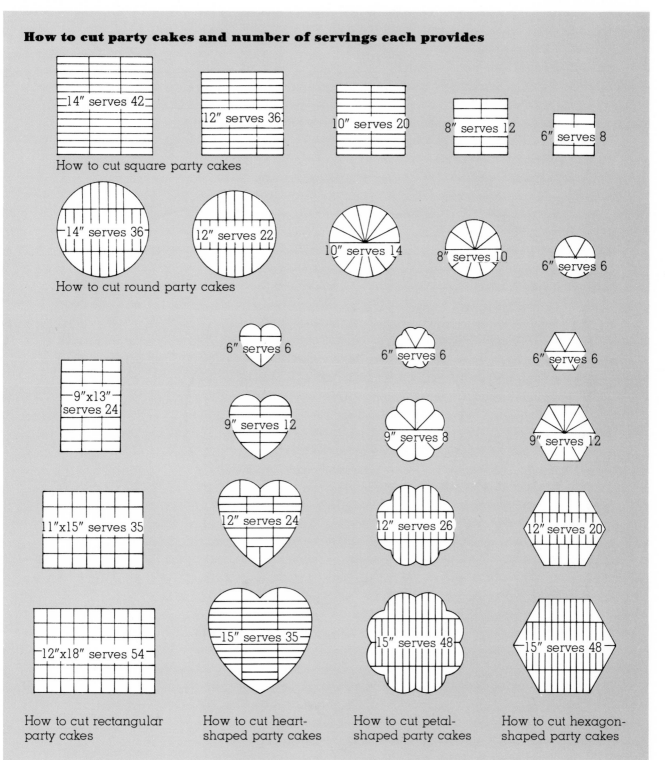

14" serves 42

12" serves 36

10" serves 20

8" serves 12

6" serves 8

How to cut square party cakes

14" serves 36

12" serves 22

10" serves 14

8" serves 10

6" serves 6

How to cut round party cakes

6" serves 6

6" serves 6

6" serves 6

9"x13" serves 24

9" serves 12

9" serves 8

9" serves 12

11"x15" serves 35

12" serves 24

12" serves 26

12" serves 20

12"x18" serves 54

15" serves 35

15" serves 48

15" serves 48

How to cut rectangular party cakes

How to cut heart-shaped party cakes

How to cut petal-shaped party cakes

How to cut hexagon-shaped party cakes

All the patterns needed for cakes in this book

To use these patterns, first accurately trace them with a hard pencil on a piece of parchment paper.

For a Color Flow design like the Love cake on page 57, tape the pattern to a piece of plexiglass or glass or a stiff board, and tape wax paper smoothly over it. Then proceed to outline and fill in. After drying, cut wax paper from surface with a sharp knife, place a piece of soft foam over the design and turn over. Carefully peel wax paper from back of design. Use the same procedure for other designs done off the cake, like the large snowflakes on the cake on page 58.

For designs piped on the cake, first let the icing crust. Pin the traced pattern to the cake, then outline with closely spaced pin pricks through the tracing. The anniversary couple on page 68 is an example.

Save your traced patterns in a folder. Then they'll be ready to use on another cake, for another party.

GIVE DAD YOUR LOVE, page 8

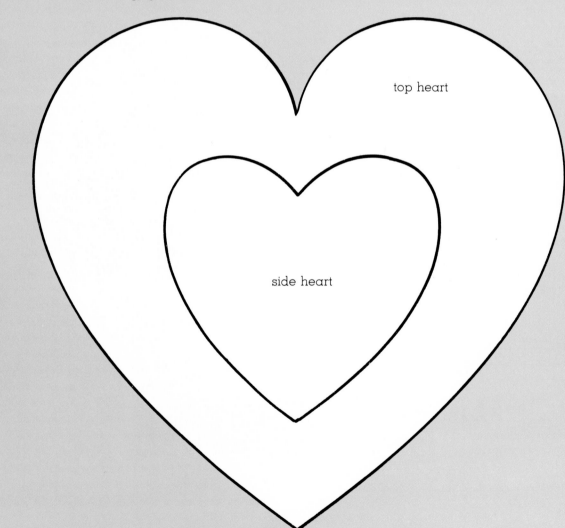

top heart

side heart

CHOCOLATE ROSE, page 8

side border pattern

ROSEBUDS, page 131

one-half of cake-top pattern

ABCDEF
GHIJKLM
NOPQRS
TUVWX
YZ&?!12
34567
890

JOLLY CLOWN, page 10

alphabet

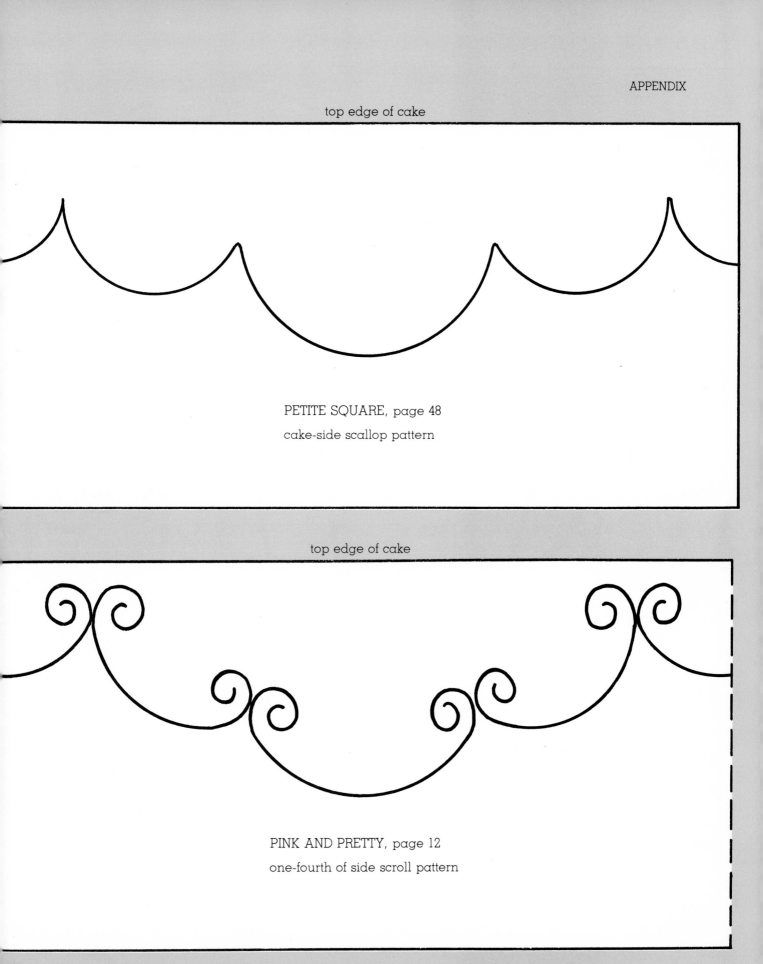

top edge of cake

PETITE SQUARE, page 48

cake-side scallop pattern

top edge of cake

PINK AND PRETTY, page 12

one-fourth of side scroll pattern

SPELL OUT LOVE, page 57

cake-top pattern

SPARKLING SNOWFLAKE, page 58

large snowflake for top

small side snowflakes

169

HAPPY FACES, page 68

Mrs. pattern

Mr. pattern

top design

HEARTS AND FLOWERS, page 65

curved side design

join broken lines
for complete pattern

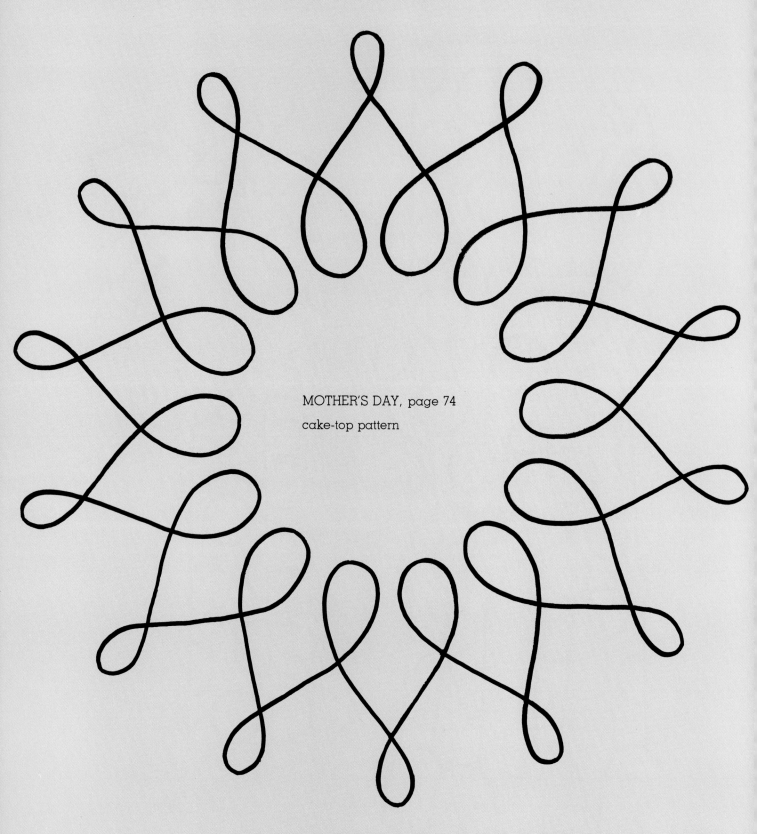

MOTHER'S DAY, page 74

cake-top pattern

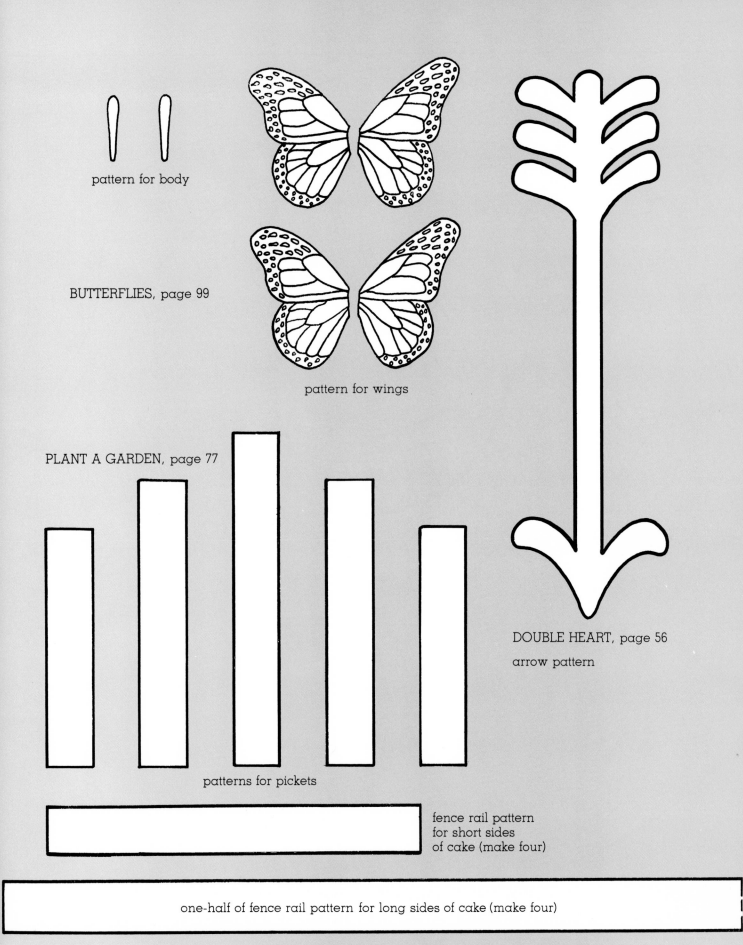

pattern for body

BUTTERFLIES, page 99

pattern for wings

PLANT A GARDEN, page 77

DOUBLE HEART, page 56

arrow pattern

patterns for pickets

fence rail pattern
for short sides
of cake (make four)

one-half of fence rail pattern for long sides of cake (make four)

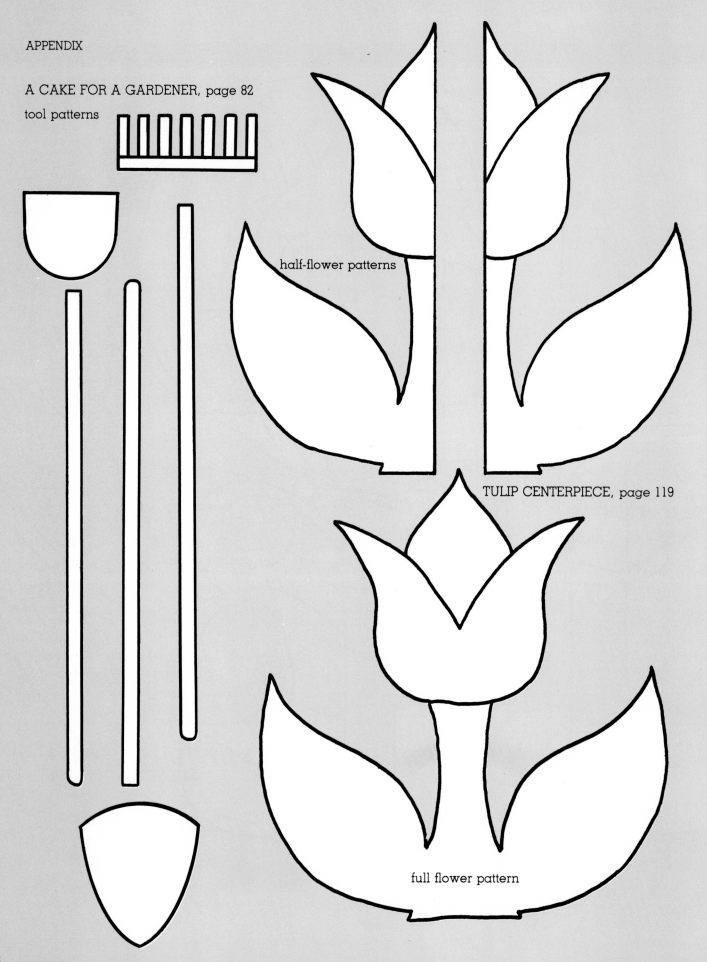

A CAKE FOR A GARDENER, page 82

tool patterns

half-flower patterns

TULIP CENTERPIECE, page 119

full flower pattern

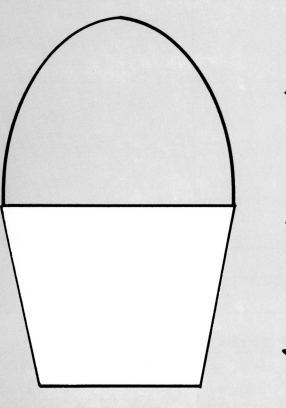

DAINTY FLOWER BASKETS, page 143

basket pattern

BIRTHDAY CARD, page 134

greeting pattern

APPENDIX

WINTER'S SNOW-WHITE CAKE, page 148

patterns for tier sides

half-stars

whole star

pattern for top ornament

pattern for tops of tiers

WEDDING WALTZ, page 159

side pattern for 10″ tier

PERFECT POINSETTIA, page 117

petal patterns

INDEX